Fukuzawa Yukichi, 1876 (Meiji 9)

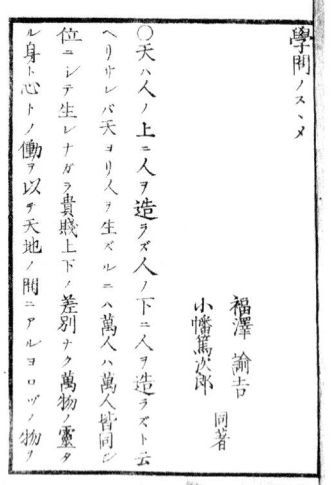

The cover (right) and the first page (left) of Section One of *An Encouragement of Learning*, published as a pamphlet in 1873 (third edition. The first edition was originally published in 1872).

An Encouragement of Learning (pp. 2–3)

The frontispiece: All images are reproduced with the permission of the Fukuzawa Memorial Center for Modern Japanese Studies, Keio University.

An Encouragement of Learning

The Thought of Fukuzawa
Volume 2

ADVISORY BOARD
Albert M. Craig
Anzai Yūichirō
Fukuzawa Takeshi
Hattori Reijirō
Sakamoto Tatsuya

EDITORIAL COMMITTEE
Helen Ballhatchet
Ikeda Yukihiro
Iwatani Jūrō
Komuro Masamichi
Nishikawa Shunsaku
Nishizawa Naoko
Yamauchi Keita

The Thought of Fukuzawa 2

Fukuzawa Yukichi

An Encouragement of Learning

Translated by
David A. Dilworth

Introduction by
Nishikawa Shunsaku

KEIO UNIVERSITY PRESS

The Thought of Fukuzawa, Volume 2
Fukuzawa Yukichi, *An Encouragement of Learning*
Published in commemoration of the sesquicentennial of Keio-gijuku

KEIO UNIVERSITY PRESS
2-19-30 Mita, Minato-ku, Tokyo 108-8346, Japan

First published as seventeen pamphlets from 1872 to 1876.
First translation into English by David A. Dilworth and Umeyo Hirano,
published by *Monumenta Nipponica*/Sophia University Press in 1969.
Revised translation in 2012 by David A. Dilworth.

Copyright © 2012 Keio University Press
All rights reserved
ISBN 978-4-7664-1684-8

Printed in Japan

CONTENTS

TRANSLATOR'S NEW FOREWORD AND ACKNOWLEDGMENTS	ix
INTRODUCTION by NISHIKAWA SHUNSAKU	xiii
A NOTE ON THE TEXT	xxxi

Section ONE   3

Section TWO   11
    Foreword
    The Equality of Men

Section THREE   19
    The Equality of Nations
    National Independence Through
      Personal Independence

Section FOUR   27
    The Duty of Scholars

Section FIVE   37
    Speech Delivered 1 January 1874

Section SIX   43
     The Importance of National Laws

Section SEVEN   51
     The Duties of the Citizens of the Nation

Section EIGHT   59
     Respect for the Independence of Others

Section NINE   67
     A Letter to Old Friends in Nakatsu Stating
        Two Ways of Learning

Section TEN   73
     Letter to Old Friends in Nakatsu, *Continued*

Section ELEVEN   79
     The Falsity of the Idea of Moral Subordination

Section TWELVE   87
     An Encouragement of Public Speaking
     The Refinement of Conduct

Section THIRTEEN   93
     The Damage of Envy in Society

Section FOURTEEN   101
     A Criticism of People's Thoughts
     The Meaning of the Word *Sewa*

Section FIFTEEN   109
     Methodic Doubt and Selective Judgment

Section SIXTEEN   119
     The Spirit of Independence in Everyday Affairs
     The Compatibility of Intention and Activity

Section SEVENTEEN 125
    On Popularity

Appendix
  A Defense of *Gakumon no Susume* 135
  Chronology of Japanese history, with special reference to
    Fukuzawa Yukichi and *An Encouragement of Learning* 147
  Fukuzawa Yukichi: Some Representative Writings *and*
    Further Reading 150

Index 153

TRANSLATOR'S NEW FOREWORD AND ACKNOWLEDGMENTS

Among his acclaimed collections, the 20th-century Japanese artist Hirayama Ikuo produced a series of paintings depicting the monk Xuanzang (602–664) and fellow Buddhist pilgrims, with their camels carrying precious cargoes of Mahayana sutras, as they crossed the searing sands, high mountain-passes, and deep valleys from India to China. The story of these arduous "west-east" journeys along the Silk Road, and of the following decades of translation of the teachings of the Dharma into Chinese—in due course affecting a significant penetration into the East Asian cultural matrix—remains as a preeminent example of efficacious "globalization" in premodern history. The influence of this cross-cultural passage was to have a far-reaching impact on the internal latticing of Japanese cultural history, and, through Japan, extends to our ever complexifying world-civilization today.

Without too much of a stretch of the historical imagination, the career of Fukuzawa Yukichi (1835–1901) can be considered to have contributed to the dynamics of inter-civilizational encounters analogous to that of Xuanzang. His three storm-tossed voyages before the Meiji Restoration to the United States and to Europe—and subsequent self-appointed mission of producing informative writings to a Japanese people cut off by thousands of miles of uncharted oceans to the West and hemmed in by hundred of years of national seclusion at home—

now symbolize another potentially momentous set of globalizing initiations. In retrospect we see that he flourished at a tipping point. Moreover, he accomplished what arguably remains peerless in comparison with any contemporary Asian or Western writer of the 19th and even possibly of the 20th centuries: his career profile consists of the twin credentials of being a prescient Japanese nationalist and the first, substantively speaking, international historian and East-West philosopher.

Fukuzawa even achieved a degree of self-consciousness of his historically maieutic role. As a leader among the pioneers of Westernization in the early years of the Meiji Period, he expressed an uncanny sense of "the trend of the times." With that sensitivity he succeeded in writing the philosophical script for the multi-layered modernization of Japan in the late 19th century. But again, adapting the phrase of Ralph Waldo Emerson, we are entitled to call Fukuzawa a Representative Man, whose descriptive, theoretical, and journalistic writings prognosticated exemplary transformations of the cultural symbolics of a range of the world's civilizations in their modernizing phases.

Chief among Fukuzawa's representative writings is *Gakumon no susume* (An Encouragement of Learning), a collection of 17 pamphlets he published during the crucial early Meiji Period years of 1872–76. Fukuzawa wrote this best-selling work at a popular level, and there is every reason to believe its charming simplicity and clarity of message remains universally attractive today. It takes time to appreciate the world-formative character of the great classics; in a hundred and fifty years Fukuzawa's *An Encouragement of Learning* is even now gaining its place among the permanent legacies of Asian intellectual history. Like one of the high mountains passed by Xuanzang and his fellow Buddhist monks, it looms larger as it recedes in the distance.

The present translation is a thorough revision of an earlier co-translation published by Sophia University Press in 1969. While doing research in Japan in 1968–69 on the philosophy of Nishida Kitaro, my Wheel of Fortune turned in the form of a cherished Japanese language instructor, Ms. Hirano Umeyo, having just retired to the Kyoto area from her years of teaching at Columbia University. We discovered that we shared a curiosity for Fukuzawa, whose handsome photo appeared on the 10,000 yen note of Japanese currency; and this led to a back-and-forth project of translating his *Gakumon no susume*.† Adding to the pleasure and instruction of this activity, about the same time I had another serendipitous turn of fortune in sharing an appetite for Fukuzawa with a fellow Columbia University scholar sojourning in Kyoto, G. C. Hurst, III. In due course our collegial conversations generated a similar "side project" of translating Fukuzawa's companion work, *Bunmeiron no gairyaku* (An Outline of a Theory of Civilization, 1875). This co-translation was eventually published by Sophia University Press in 1973; and it happily reappeared in an updated revision by Keio University Press in 2008. Each of these original "Kyoto" translations received a significant boost from the expertise of Edmund R. Skrzypczak, then editor of *Monumenta Nipponica* and Sophia University Press, and his staff member, Mr. Sawada Tetsuya.‡

The original "Kyoto" co-translations of almost forty years ago of Fukuzawa's principal philosophical works have thus been reborn in these present two "Tokyo" redactions. They are the result of several years of gracious encouragement from Mr. Sakagami Hiroshi, Chairman of Keio University Press, and of sustained interaction with his brilliant staff, principally among whom were Ms. Katahara Ryoko, who took over the revision of *Gakumon no susume*, and Ms. Nagano Fumika, who first edited the revision of *Bunmeiron*. Following the meticulous editorial pattern established by Ms. Nagano, Ms. Katahara, with her own care and competence, ensured the precision of this revised translation of *Gakumon*, while improving the overall value of the volume through the addition of apt historical footnotes, chronologies, primary and secondary source bibliographies, and an expanded index. Professor Helen Ballhatchet of Keio University also contributed her historian's expertise

---

† *Gakumon no susume* came out originally as a series of pamphlets begun in 1872 and completed in 1876. According to Fukuzawa, the first pamphlet (Section One in this translation) including a pirated version sold 220,000 copies. In a total Japanese population of around 35 million in the 1870s, one out of every 160 persons must have bought it, and presumably even more had read it. His earlier work, *Seiyō jijō* (Conditions in the West, 1866), was another bestseller which had a similar impact upon the mind of his times.

‡ Fukuzawa Yukichi, *An Outline of a Theory of Civilization*, trans. David A. Dilworth and G. Cameron Hurst III, with an introduction by Inoki Takenori, Keio University Press, 2008, reissued by Columbia University Press in 2009.

to our staff discussions of the text.

In this regard, our translation committee was also blessed to have had the gracious participation of the renowned Fukuzawa scholar, Professor Emeritus Nishikawa Shunsaku of Keio University; and the present volume has the added value of featuring his authoritative Introduction. As he informs us, his Introduction is itself a revision of an original UNESCO paper which he updated after he very recently discovered new materials in Fukuzawa's papers. Professor Nishikawa's informative Introduction is of interest for having been originally written to introduce Fukuzawa in general, not especially focused upon *An Encouragement of Learning*, but therefore framing the latter work in broader context and perspective.

In preparing this version of the translation I was privileged to have it reviewed by Professor Albert M. Craig, who kindly provided his comments and advice. I should also like to express my appreciation for the contribution of Professor Komuro Masamichi of Keio University for checking the chronologies appended to the translation.

It has been a personal pleasure to have shared in bringing this revised translation of Fukuzawa's most famous work to an international readership. *An Encouragement of Learning* sparkles with Fukuzawa's brilliance that comes from his fresh experiences and keen powers of observation. With his remarkable gift for wit and satire, it radiates with his sense of real problems, priorities, and solutions. It is the legacy of an East Asian Representative Man, who was at once philosopher, educator, and moralist, uniquely alive to the pulse of his times and keenly aware of the positive potentialities of world-historical change. He dealt in the currency of the will to learn rather than the will to believe. Even now we are his students, receiving his encouragement to learn.

David A. Dilworth
Philosophy Department
State University of New York at Stony Brook

INTRODUCTION

The Life and Works of Fukuzawa Yukichi[†]

In Japan, a portrait of Fukuzawa Yukichi appears on every 10,000-yen note. This is official recognition of his dedication to the cause of introducing Western institutions and thought into Japan. Some people, however, may wonder why he wears traditional Japanese robes. Although there are a number of pictures of Fukuzawa, only a few are in Western attire. It seems that this reflects his basic stance: he always emphasized the spiritual revolution rather than the spurious imitation of things Western.

Fukuzawa first learned Dutch and later changed to English studies; he visited the United States twice and traveled through Europe for almost a year before the Meiji Restoration (1868). On these journeys he was able to perceive the basic "corner-stones and pillars" of modern society developing in the West. There he also conceived his manifest destiny—education and journalism. Soon after his second voyage he began to set up his school, the Keio-gijuku, which was to produce many talented graduates in business, industry, and politics.

Fukuzawa published numerous pamphlets and textbooks that were

---

[†] This introduction was originally published as "Fukuzawa Yukichi" in *Prospects: the Quarterly Review of Comparative Education* (UNESCO: International Bureau of Education, vol. XXIII, no. 3/4, 1993, pp. 493–506). I reproduce it here with courtesy of UNESCO, with some further reflections on Fukuzawa I have had in more recent years.

used in Japan's emerging modern schools and were also welcomed by a variety of other types of reader. The great attraction of these writings was not only that the topics were new, but that their style was revolutionary in its simplicity. The Japanese people were able to learn much about their forthcoming advance to modern civilization from the so-called "Fukuzawa books."

Fukuzawa also wrote many books and articles for scholars. These were mostly published by the university press or through the newspaper he launched in 1882, *Jiji-shinpō* (The Times). From that time on, Fukuzawa wrote numerous articles and satires on such contemporary issues as politics, international relations, economic and financial problems, educational policy, women's rights, and a moral code.

His main theme may be summarized in one word—independence—based on his conviction that personal and national independence constituted the real foundation of modern society in the West. In order for Japan to achieve a comparable level of independence, Fukuzawa advocated Western, or practical and scientific, learning, instead of the traditional studies of the Chinese classics. The more educated the people became, the better their national independence could be achieved, with a corresponding increase in public virtue and social morality.

Although Fukuzawa evidently learned much from Western thinkers, he was not blindly attached to Western civilization. He was well aware of its flaws, but realized that Western civilization was technologically superior to the Japanese situation, and so he concluded that the Japanese people should use it as a model. He seemed, however, to have anticipated the difficulties that arose in revolutionizing the minds of his countrymen.

Boyhood and Student Days

Fukuzawa was born in Osaka in 1835. This was a period that had been preceded by two centuries of isolation from the rest of the world. It was to be followed nineteen years later by the opening up of Japan, a timeframe during which the governing bodies of the Tokugawa Shogunate and the 260 domains that had held power for so long were trying desperately to adjust to the profound political and economic changes, including chronic suffering caused by budget deficits, taking place in society.

Fukuzawa's family lived in Osaka, which at that time was the trading center of Japan. His father worked as a low-level treasury officer representing his home domain of Nakatsu (a province in the northern part of the island of Kyushu). His class in society was that of samurai, but of low rank with a modest hereditary position. The job did not appeal to Fukuzawa's father, but he remained loyally in service until his sudden death at the age of 44, barely eighteen months after the birth of Fukuzawa.

The widowed mother returned to Nakatsu to bring up her two sons and three daughters. Their allowance reduced them to poverty, and they were obliged to supplement their income with casual paid work in the home. The young Fukuzawa repaired sandals and did other odd jobs. There was no money to send him to school until he was 14, ten years after the usual starting age.

Elementary education at the time was divided between one type of school for male children of samurai, and another for children of commoners. Sons of samurai, aged 5-7, learned the Chinese classics from either their father or some relative and then from masters of Neo-Confucian Learning, who often ran private classes or schools. Secondary and/or higher education was provided either in private schools or in the domain school. Since the mid-eighteenth century, most of the large domains had inaugurated domain schools. The domain of Nakatsu had its own school, but entry was restricted, the rank of the student's family being an important factor. The son of a low-ranking samurai, even if he were the eldest, did not qualify for enrollment in a domain school.

The learning available inside an isolated Tokugawa Japan was limited by government decree, but to imagine Japan as totally cut off would be to oversimplify. Westerners had reached the shores of Japan ever since the sixteenth century, but they had been barred entry in the early 1640s, when only Dutch traders were allowed to stay on the small man-made island of Dejima in Nagasaki harbor. This contact with the outside world was tightly controlled by the Shogun and special permission was required for merchants, interpreters, and military personnel to go to Dejima.

Nonetheless, Western knowledge, especially medical and natural science, somehow filtered through the Shogun's barriers and was diffused throughout the country. Eighty years before Fukuzawa's time, several Japanese physicians had pioneered the translation of the Dutch version of J. A. Kulumus' *Tabulae anatomicae* (Ontleedkundige tafalen). The commodity of Western Learning was in limited supply, strictly controlled, and sometimes constituted a danger for its students, but it existed nevertheless.

Fukuzawa soon revealed his ability at school. But while he excelled inside the classroom, outside of it his low rank left him vulnerable. When playing with his upper-samurai classmates, the lower-ranking Fukuzawa was the brunt of their arrogance. Upper and lower pedigrees were still strict enough to prohibit marriages between the two groups. Even as a young man Fukuzawa came deeply to resent the inequality of the system.[†]

The arrival of Admiral Perry's fleet in the summer of 1853 sent a profound shock throughout the country—to samurai and commoner alike. For Fukuzawa it meant that he was asked by his brother (who had inherited his father's position) to go to Nagasaki to learn Dutch in order to master Western gunnery. The elder brother wished to give Fukuzawa a unique opportunity and prospect of rendering a service to his lord in the future. Fukuzawa accepted his suggestion with no real understanding of what Dutch was or what threat was represented from the outside—he was, however, most anxious to leave his home town.

They left for Nagasaki one month before the Treaty of Peace and Amity between Japan and the United States (March 1854). Fukuzawa became a servant/student to the councilor of the lord of Nakatsu's heir, who was there for the same purpose. Though they were hardly able to learn the alphabet there, they were transferred to the "master" of gunnery who really did not understand Dutch very well either. The councilor's son eventually became jealous of Fukuzawa. He falsified a letter which fabricated a story that Fukuzawa's mother was ill in Nakatsu, and suggested that Fukuzawa return home. Fukuzawa discovered the

---

† Fukuzawa gives a first-hand account of the rank structure of samurai retainers of his domain. See his article, "Kyū-han-jō," translated by Carmen Backer in *Monumenta Nipponica*, vol. 9, no. 1 (Tokyo: Sophia University, 1953).

falsehood but decided to leave Nagasaki anyway. Having no money, he forged the signature of an official and charged his expenses to the domain warehouse in Osaka. Instead of returning for home, he headed for Edo (now Tokyo), 1,000 kilometers to the north, to continue his studies.

The boat trip across the Inland Sea was to take two weeks owing to its numerous stops. En route, Fukuzawa decided to disembark and walked through the night to reach the Osaka domain warehouse where his brother, Sannosuke, was stationed. Sannosuke persuaded Fukuzawa to stay and enroll in a Dutch-language school, the Teki-juku, which was run by a physician, Ogata Kōan (1810-63). Ogata did not teach medicine exclusively; he was also successful in distributing vaccines in Japan and in educating many young men like Fukuzawa who would later play roles in the building of the modern nation.

Well into Fukuzawa's three-year stay at the Teki-juku, both he and his older brother fell ill and were sent back to Nakatsu to recover. Sannosuke died there. As he had no experience as a treasurer to take over his father's old job, Fukuzawa was to succeed Sannosuke in performing guard duty at the Nakatsu castle. He begged his mother to let him return again to study at the Teki-juku and subsequently received official permission to do so.

In the next year, Fukuzawa became the top student at the school and his autobiography recalls fond memories of these schooldays in Osaka.[†] He and his colleagues mainly studied physics, chemistry, and physiology, and copied and translated a Dutch book on the art of fort-building.

The Move to the Capital and to the World

In the autumn of 1858, Fukuzawa was appointed teacher of Dutch to the vassals of the domain of Nakatsu. The course was to be held in the second domain house of Edo. This time Fukuzawa travelled on foot to Edo with "real money" and a servant. This "servant" was actually Okamoto Setsuzō (1837-77), one of his colleagues who later completed

---

† *The Autobiography of Yukichi Fukuzawa*, trans. Eiichi Kiyooka (Columbia University Press, 2006).

the translation of a statistical table giving figures about the nations of the world.†

July 1859 marked the opening of three ports in Japan according to terms of the Treaty of Amity and Commerce that had been signed in the previous year with the United States and some European nations. Soon after the opening of the ports, Fukuzawa went to visit Kanagawa (now Yokohama) where he was disappointed to find that he could not read the signs or make himself understood. English and not Dutch was the language of the port cities. He then decided to learn English, but he made slow progress since he could find neither a good teacher nor a good dictionary.

At this time when, within the terms of the Treaty, the Shogunate decided to dispatch envoys to the United States, Fukuzawa seized the opportunity to volunteer his services to Admiral Kimura Yoshitake (1830-1901). After thirty-seven days at sea on a voyage marked by consecutive storms, they reached San Francisco in the spring of 1860. During his one-month stay, Fukuzawa's most significant acquisitions were a Webster's dictionary and a photograph of himself with the photographer's daughter. This dictionary, recommended by the interpreter, John Manjirō,‡ is deemed to have been Fukuzawa's first intellectual weapon in understanding modern civilization.

After his return, Fukuzawa was employed in the foreign affairs office of the Shogunate in translating diplomatic documents. The next year he married O-kin, the daughter of an upper-rank samurai from his home domain. In 1867 Fukuzawa was able to go to the United States for a second time. The mission visited Washington, D.C. and New York to negotiate on the unsettled purchase of a warship from the United States Government. Fukuzawa's real priority was to acquire textbooks for students who were forced to copy their foreign texts by hand. He bought as many books as possible within his budget.

---

† P. A. de Jong (publisher), *Statistische tafel van alle landen der aarde*, Arnhem, 1854.
‡ John Manjirō (1827–98) was a Japanese fisherman. When his ship went adrift in the Pacific in 1841, the crews were rescued by an American whaling ship. Manjirō was brought to the USA, where he studied English and navigation, and worked for years on a whaling boat as well as in a gold mine, to make enough money to go back to Japan in 1851. In 1860 he returned to America aboard the *Kanrinmaru*, the ship which carried the first Japanese government delegation members that also included Fukuzawa Yukichi.

Fukuzawa's most important voyage was his second, in 1862, when he accompanied a mission to Europe, whose assignment was to negotiate the postponement of additional port openings and to secure an adjustment of the exchange rate. The official mission failed on both accounts, but Fukuzawa managed to travel to France, the United Kingdom, the Netherlands, Germany, Russia, and Portugal. In his capacity as translator, he observed many new things and institutions such as hospitals, arsenals, mines and schools. Based on what he saw and read in this year-long tour, Fukuzawa published the first volume of his *Seiyō jijō* (The Conditions in the West), which became a national bestseller.

Fukuzawa realized that technical progress was an essential component of the prosperity he witnessed in Europe. He believed that a revolution in people's knowledge and thinking was a fundamental requirement for similar progress in Japan. While in London, he sent a letter to a friend at home stating that the most urgent thing to do was to educate talented young people in things Western rather than to purchase machinery and armaments. He decided to postpone the writing of the second volume of *Seiyō jijō* and instead translated John Hill Burton's *Political Economy*. In this 1867 book, to which he gave the title *The Outside Volume* (Gaihen), he focused upon the "corner-stones and main pillars," that is to say, the intangible social network, constituting civilized society.† It was in effect another introduction to "the condition of the West."

After his return to Japan, Fukuzawa began to set up his own school. The student body grew rapidly to 100 by 1867. His duties with the Shogunate were only six days a month, a circumstance that enabled him to use the other days for reading, writing, and teaching. The popularity of his accounts of Western life indicated interest and tolerance of the outside world. There were other groups, however, who wanted to expel the "barbarians" together with any Japanese scholars interested in Western studies. The fanatic *jōi rōnin* (breakaway groups of samurai who

---

† More exactly, the first part of *The Outside Volume* (supplementary volume), discussing 'social economy,' is a translation of *Political Economy for Use in Schools, and for Private Instruction* (Edinburgh, 1852). Albert M. Craig, in "John Hill Burton and Fukuzawa Yukichi" (*Kindai Nihon Kenkyū* 1, Tokyo, 1984), has identified the work as having been written by John Hill Burton in the series "Chamber's Educational Course," published by William and Robert Chambers. See also Albert M. Craig, *Civilization and Enlightenment: The Early Thought of Fukuzawa Yukichi* (Cambridge: Harvard University Press, 2009).

wanted to expel foreigners) were apt to murder those who represented Western ideals. People like Fukuzawa were at risk. In fact Ōmura Masujirō (born in 1820), undersecretary of the Emperor's army, was killed by them in 1869.

The Encouragement of Learning

In this tense atmosphere, and amid the sounds of gunfire from a battle only a few kilometers from Keio-gijuku, Fukuzawa continued his lectures on political economy as usual.† It was 4 July 1868 and the Restoration forces were challenging the tottering Tokugawa regime. Fukuzawa told his students, reduced from 100 to 18 on that day, "Whatever happens in the country, whatever warfare harasses our land, we will never relinquish our commitment to Western Learning. As long as this school of ours stands, Japan has become a civilized nation of the world" (*The Autobiography*).

These words explain clearly what Fukuzawa had in mind—Western Learning and education. Soon after the defeat of the Tokugawa forces in Edo, the new authorities asked Fukuzawa to join the government service. He declined the offer and never became a partisan of the new government, a decision which gave him much more freedom in judging and writing about the course of the emerging political parties. In the years that followed, he devoted himself exclusively to teaching at Keio-gijuku and to helping initiate modern schools elsewhere. He also translated and/or wrote pamphlets about the West and elementary textbooks on a surprisingly wide variety of subjects, including physics, geography, military arts, the British Parliament, and international relations.

Among his books, *Gakumon no susume* (An Encouragement of Learning) is the most celebrated. It was originally a series of pamphlets written and published between 1872 and 1876. The first essay, which

---

† The textbook was *Elements of Political Economy* (Boston, 1835), many copies of which Fukuzawa had purchased in New York or Washington in 1867. The author of the book was an American clergyman, Francis Wayland (1796–1865), who was President of Brown University. He also published another college textbook on *Moral Science* that was read by Fukuzawa and his fellows in 1869 and afterwards.

achieved an enormous success, was the manifestation of Fukuzawa's thesis to the general public. The opening lines read: "Heaven, it is said, does not create one person above or below another. [...] the question of the difference between wise and stupid is traceable to the degree of learning" (p. 3)

What is important here is Fukuzawa's concept of education—the "practical learning that is closer to ordinary human needs," or, in a word *jitsugaku*. In his judgment it consisted first of learning the forty-seven Japanese *kana* syllabary, the methods of accounting and the abacus, the ways to use weights and measures and, after these fundamentals, such subjects as geography, physics, history, economics, and ethics.

The subjects in the first group had been taught in the *terakoya*, which literally means "temple school." Since the sixteenth century the *terakoya*'s connection with Buddhism had gradually diminished. In the next century it became a primary school for commoners' children and daughters of samurai, particularly those of low rank; the teachers of were such people as poor samurai, village headmen, or Shinto priests. Buddhist teachers were rather scarce in the eighteenth century. The *terakoya* continued to mushroom in the first half of the nineteenth century. Aware of this, Fukuzawa chose to put more emphasis on the subjects in the second group, those areas that were more developed in the West than in the East, in his modernized education program.

Along with this orientation he sharply criticized the traditional Japanese school curriculum, which emphasized the study of ancient texts and the enjoyment and writing of poetry, as providing impractical pursuits. He argued for the necessity of Western education, urging boys and girls who had just learned *kana* letters to consult translated textbooks and, at a more advanced stage, to learn to read the Western language editions. In his own school he relied on Western authors, and by 1890 had hired foreign teachers.

Fukuzawa felt that *jitsugaku* would contribute to personal independence, but that "freedom and independence refer not only to the private individual, but to the nation as well." Believing that these elements were human rights, he famously concluded:

[T]he principle of Heaven grants freedom from bondage to each individual person, and each individual country is free from bondage as well. Consequently, if there is some threat which might infringe upon a country's freedom, that country should not hesitate to take up arms against all the countries of the world. (pp. 7-8)

It can be understood from this why he also translated military manuals.

Fukuzawa's style in *An Encouragement of Learning* and in other textbooks and manuals was completely new to Japan. In the past, books had been written in a Chinese script with characters difficult for ordinary people to understand. His ingenuous style was colloquial and comprehensible even for the less educated. In the face of the general skeptical opinion that the Japanese language did not lend itself to oratory, he started public speaking and conducted open debates. He built a meeting hall at Keio-gijuku where he, his colleagues, and students held many gatherings and debating contests. This small building, the Enzetsukan, still stands on the campus at Mita.

The Theory of Civilization

In a letter dated 23 February 1874 to one of the Keio fellows, Shōda Heigorō (1847-1922), Fukuzawa wrote:

> I don't think I'll take on any more translations. This year I'm going to read and work without worrying about the hundreds of miscellaneous things. My health is getting better, and my knowledge will be exhausted unless I study more. I shall spend about a year on my studies.

This was in anticipation of reading the references and drafting his *magnum opus*, *Bunmeiron no gairyaku* (An Outline of a Theory of Civilization), which appeared the following year.†

---

† After I wrote this article, Fukuzawa's own "A Plan for *An Outline of a Theory of Civilization*" (dated 25 February 1874) was discovered in his papers. As he published *An Outline* as a monograph in August of 1875, this suggests that he began to write it, as well as a dozen sections of *An Encouragement of Learning*, in the course of years prior to 1874.

Unlike the other works by Fukuzawa, which were mainly for public consumption, this book was intended for Japanese intellectuals. At that time the intelligentsia were divided into several camps—some were very enthusiastic about introducing an ideal Western model of civilization, others were dragging their feet or even opposed to modern values and principles. Fukuzawa wanted to clarify the terms of the argument and to persuade them to present a common front in favor of modernity.

While Fukuzawa was a prolific writer who produced an enormous quantity of work, it took an exceptional effort to finish this book. The manuscripts, which are preserved today, show that he revised them again and again. The style was scholarly and hence not so easy to read, at times eloquent, and presenting all points of view. Nonetheless, his main theme was crystal clear: self-sufficiency and national independence. "Civilization" was both the end and the means to independence.

What, then, is "civilization"?

> In its broad sense "civilization" means not only comfort in daily necessities but also the refining of knowledge and the cultivation of virtue so as to elevate human life to a higher plane. . . . [Thus] it refers to the attainment of *both* material well-being *and* the elevation of the human spirit. . . . [But] since what produces man's well-being and refinement is knowledge and virtue, civilization ultimately means the progress of man's knowledge and virtue. (pp. 45-48)

Fukuzawa then took great pains to distinguish knowledge and virtue. He defined virtue as morality, and knowledge as intelligence, adding that in English they are termed "morals" and "intellect," respectively. He specified these definitions so as to avoid any association with Neo-Confucian concepts and to signal his break with traditional thinking.

Traditional Japanese teaching promoted private virtue and benevolent rule as imparted by the Chinese classics. Overall, the classics were concerned mainly with the art of governing—the exemplary ruler, usually the king or emperor, benevolently governing his people and land by his personal competence and virtue. The people, on the other hand, remained uneducated and dependent on the ruler. Most traditional Japanese scholars, in both official and private academies, taught young people how to read, but they did not encourage any original thought or novel ideas. The courses had nothing to do with political economy: such subjects were considered either "vulgar" or inappropriate for the young. Teaching in *terakoya* was assuredly practical, but not very scientific. Knowledge gained there at best only contributed to personal intellect and profit.

As indicated above, Buddhism in Japan had lost its authority and educational function in the previous centuries. Buddhist believers had become mere subjects of the political authority, namely the Tokugawa Shogunate. Thus, not only the Neo-Confucian scholars and Buddhists but also the commoners and samurai depended on their hereditary positions. Most of them were indifferent to public matters. They were governed by, credulous of, and blindly faithful to the ruler upon whom all the power was vested. In Fukuzawa's estimation, this was the most radically negative feature of Japanese civilization.

In Fukuzawa's thinking, virtue and knowledge could each be divided into two parts, private and public. He was convinced that every person has an innate integrity and potential talent. But while it was quite possible to acquire private knowledge in school, it was impossible to make a person use his private virtue publicly. Looking at history, he saw that the ruled had their virtue bottled up inside them: it could rarely surface—at best, only within the family unit. Private knowledge, on the other hand, could be transformed into public knowledge or wisdom. People had begun to recognize empirical laws and science, and not only the natural but also moral (or social) sciences. "In Western civilization," Fukuzawa wrote, "the social fabric includes various theories that have developed side by side, have drawn closer to one another, and finally united into one fabric of civilization—in the process giving birth to freedom and independence." Thus while Japanese thinking had been concentrating on the impossible task of creating public virtue, the West had progressed in the trajectory of public knowledge or wisdom. That is why he revered Western Learning and criticized Neo-Confucian teaching in his country.

In this regard, Japanese civilization lagged behind the West. Adopting the theory of human development as having advanced in stages from "barbarous" to "half-civilized" to "civilized," he placed Japan (along with China) in the half-civilized stage. Although "advanced" and "backward" are relative terms, the distance between East and West was assuredly great. Since civilization meant the development of the inner spirit, namely the virtue and knowledge, of the entire nation, it was impossible, in Fukuzawa's thinking, to be able to catch up with the more advanced nations simply by purchasing modern arms, machinery, and external structures. Hence it followed for Fukuzawa that "the Western Civilization [is] Our Goal."

In the final chapter of *An Outline of a Theory of Civilization*, Fukuzawa turned again to the problem of "national independence" which was a serious concern for all Japanese intellectuals. Japan, he believed, was in reality only a small far-Eastern country at that time, and hence did not require the support of great military power. He concluded:

> Moreover, the arguments for national polity, for Christianity, and for Confucianism . . . are all insufficient to bolster people's hearts. What, then, will? I say, there is only one thing: namely, to establish our goal and advance toward civilization. . . . [T]he way in which to preserve this independence cannot be sought anywhere except in civilization. (pp. 253-54)

Hard Years, 1877-81

The number of students at Keio-gijuku climbed back to more than 300 between 1871 and 1876, then began to decline again, in part because of the unsettled domestic scene. As most of the students were samurai, a decision by the government in 1871 to abolish domains and reduce the hereditary privileges and stipends of the lords and vassals also affected the amount of money that could be spent on education. In five years, this process of disenfranchisement of the samurai class was completed. The *shizoku* (ex-samurai and their families) were given a compensating debenture, the amount of which was modest compared with that given to the *kazoku* (aristocrats) and the higher-ranking *shizoku*. The majority of *shizoku*—the medium and lower ranks—were not satisfied with the arrangement. Only Fukuzawa was pleased to declare himself a commoner (*heimin*) and declined any compensation.

During this period, Fukuzawa's students, most of whom were samurai, had to withdraw from the school because of their lost privileges and worsening poverty due to inflation. Those who came from Satsuma returned to join the Rebellion there and were either killed or wounded. In dire financial straits, Fukuzawa supplemented the school's budget with his personal income and also asked for loans from the government and private sources. No one, however, was willing to lend the Keio-gijuku any money; some suggested that it should be dissolved. His fellow teachers responded by voluntarily offering a reduction of their salary by two-thirds. In due course, the number of students gradually recovered from a low of 200 in 1878 to as many as 500 in 1881. Interestingly, the ratio of commoners enrolled grew from a third to more than a half by 1875. Fukuzawa later conjectured that this was due to the post-war inflation that raised the wealthy farmers' incomes sufficiently to send their sons to the Keio-gijuku.

As the government was heavily dependent on fixed land taxes for its revenues, it was also suffering financial deficits. As a measure to reduce expenditure, it decided to sell government factories and enterprises. When it was announced that these properties had been sold off at incredibly low prices, civil rights leaders severely criticized the government. A rumor appeared in the press that Fukuzawa, with the financial help of Iwasaki Yatarō (1835-85) of the Mitsubishi Corporation, was urging a *coup d'état* by Ōkuma Shigenobu (1838-1922), one of the government members. In a counter move, Itō Hirobumi (1841-1909), another member of the government, purged Ōkuma from the cabinet. The real reason for this political drama was a struggle for control over input on legislation for the future constitution. The man who was able to exercise this control was expected to be the *de facto* prime-minister. Several Keio graduates who had worked under Ōkuma had suggested a constitutional monarchy on the British model, while the Ito faction preferred the Prussian type. This group was responding to, and afraid of, Fukuzawa, the Keio fellows, and students, since Fukuzawa himself often expressed active support for Ōkuma's policies.

Criticisms and Appreciation

After his political victory, Itō suspended legislating any constitution and opening of the Diet for ten years, and canceled the sale of government properties. Before their split, Itō, Okuma and other members of the government had arranged with Fukuzawa to start a newspaper to help promote the early opening of the Diet, but this too was shelved. Fukuzawa decided to proceed alone and launched his *Jiji-shinpō* on 1 March 1882. In the inaugural article, he declared that this quality newspaper would remain impartial and independent.

From that time onward most of Fukuzawa's writings, not only serious articles but also satire, appeared in the *Jiji-shinpō*. He addressed all kinds of contemporary issues—politics, domestic and international issues, political economy, education and educational policy, the moral code, particularly women's rights, and so forth. These articles and satires fill nearly half of the twenty-two volumes of his *Collected Works*.

In a broad overview of his works, it can be seen that Fukuzawa had always unswervingly advocated individual and national independence. Yet even in the 1870s there were controversies over his discussions of moral issues concerning loyalty, money matters, and so forth.[†] As well, serious criticisms have recently been leveled at his articles from the 1880s onwards. Such criticisms have insinuated serious doubts as to Fukuzawa's real intentions and his character. The brunt of the reactions had been against his articles on Japan's role in Asia. These criticisms have nearly obscured the impact of his less controversial articles—for instance, the ones about women's equality—and have placed Fukuzawa in the very category to which he had always been opposed.

One such article, and perhaps the most disputed, is his 1885 "Datsua-ron" (Departure from Asia). There Fukuzawa stated:

> Our immediate policy, therefore, should be to lose no time in waiting

---

[†] For example Sections Six and Seven caused a heated controversy, the so-called "Nankō-Gonsuke-ron." Fukuzawa's rejoinder is included in the Appendix.

for the enlightenment of our neighboring countries [Korea and China] so as to join them in developing Asia, but rather to depart from their ranks and cast our lot with the civilized countries of the West [....] We should deal with them exactly as the Westerners do.

Some readers today react strongly to this passage. Yet it can be more satisfactorily understood if it is seen in its proper context. Fukuzawa's seemingly aggressive stance against Japan's Asian neighbors reflected the changing international relations in East Asia during those years. Moreover, Fukuzawa's concern with Korea had its own history.

Fukuzawa had been acquainted with the Korean reformists, Pak Yong-hyo and Kim Ok-kyun, since 1881. Kim (1851-94) had particularly close contacts with Fukuzawa when he came to Japan three times between 1882 and 1884, receiving much advice and every assistance from Fukuzawa during his visits (each one lasting several months). Fukuzawa recommended that talented young men should be educated, that the people should be enlightened through a "newspaper," and that Korean sovereignty and independence from China should be secured.

In accordance with these recommendations, Kim, in the first instance, sent a group of young students to the Keio-gijuku, as well as to a military academy, and to other Japanese schools. Secondly, a newspaper, or more properly speaking, a governmental bulletin, was published three times a month beginning in November 1883 through the efforts of Inoue Kakugorō (1860-1938), who was dispatched to Korea by Fukuzawa in December 1882 and appointed project adviser by the king of Korea. The third objective, however, was extremely difficult to achieve; following the 1882 anti-Japanese revolt by the Korean army, China had declared her suzerainty and exercised a firm grip over the Korean court.

Fukuzawa's expectation for Korean progress faded as Korean dependence upon China grew. "Traditions" were once again the lifelong enemy of Fukuzawa. In such a hopeless situation, he saw a parting of the ways—Japan choosing change, with Korea and China resisting it. Thus a more sympathetic view of Fukuzawa's suggestion of Japan's departure from Asia can be sustained with the knowledge that, for several years, his efforts were directed at aiding enlightenment and reform in Korea. Fukuzawa's articles on Korea after 1881 were numerous, but always emphasizing its sovereignty and national independence. On the contrary, in "Departure from Asia," he criticized Chinese imperialism and rejected giving China any special consideration simply on the grounds that it was a neighboring country.

Fukuzawa's concerns for women is apparent in his main writings, and are now collected in *Fukuzawa Yukichi on Japanese Women*. From today's perspective his position on women's rights seems somewhat conservative. But no one can deny that he was the only Meiji thinker who tirelessly argued for women's equality. In addition to several earlier articles, he wrote much to the same effect in the late 1880s. His focus was directed to where the biggest problem lay in Japan—such as women's rights in the home, the growth of their independence there, as well as elimination of the their subjection to men in society.

Fukuzawa criticized the customary ill conduct of men towards women, and condemned the remaining vestiges of polygamy. Both, he argued, qualified as among the most uncivilized customs of Japanese society. Advocating fundamental equality for women and their equal ownership of the family property, he wrote:

> Therefore, to teach them [women] at least an outline of economics and law is the first requirement after giving them a general education. Figuratively speaking, it will be like providing the women of civilized society with a pocket dagger for self-protection.

Some recent comments concerning his arguments on women suggest that Fukuzawa held too narrow a view. For example, he never suggested public activism for women; he mainly encouraged middle-class women compared to those of the lower classes; he did not touch on the issue of women in the labor force (most of whom worked in wretched conditions); and, lastly, he did not condemn the prostitution of poor girls or their migration overseas, since he regarded it as preferable to starvation. Despite the limitations of Fukuzawa's definition of equality of women, considering their position in his day, his arguments were appreciated by women at the time, as is shown by the following letter passed anonymously by a lady to Mrs. Fukuzawa at the time of his funeral:

Every time I read Sensei's articles on Japanese women in *Jiji-shinpō*, I feel grateful that he is our real friend. Indeed, it is our deep sorrow to lose Sensei now [...] With my tears, I sincerely hope that Sensei's desires shall permeate our country for ever.

To sum up, in his time Fukuzawa was a *sensei* not only to boys and girls in schools but also to Japanese men and women in society at large, and he is still our teacher today.

Nishikawa Shunsaku, *Former Director*
Fukuzawa Memorial Center of Keio University
Professor Emeritus, Keio University

A NOTE ON THE TEXT

This English translation of Fukuzawa Yukichi's *Gakumon no susume* (An Encouragement of Learning) has been revised and reset from the first edition published by *Monumenta Nipponica* and Sophia University Press in 1969. In this new edition, Fukuzawa's original notes to the text are indicated with asterisks. Additional notes are indicated by daggers and given in square brackets. English words employed by Fukuzawa in the original Japanese text are shown by the use of bold face.

All Japanese names appearing in the text are written in the Japanese order, i.e. with family name followed by first name. All Japanese words are romanized according to the modified Hepburn system. Macrons have been included to indicate long syllables but have been eliminated from fully anglicized words, such as "Tokyo" or "Kyoto." With the exception of Confucius (Kong Fuzi) and Mencius (Mengzi), all Chinese names are rendered according to the Pin-yin system. The original Chinese and Japanese versions of names are given in the index.

AN ENCOURAGEMENT OF LEARNING

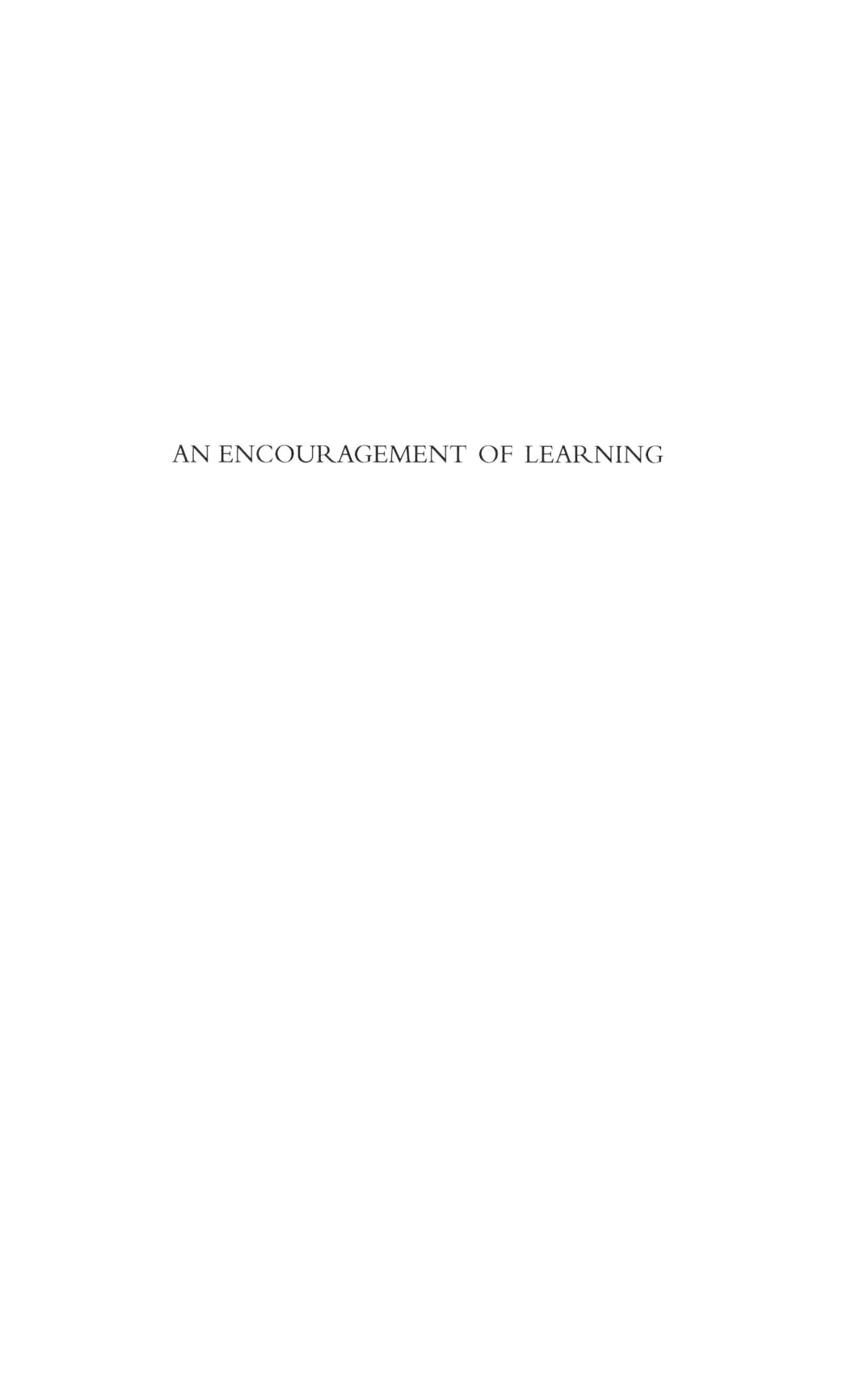

Section
ONE

H EAVEN, it is said, does not create one person above or below another. This signifies that when we are born from Heaven we all are equal and there is no innate distinction between high and low. It means that we humans, who are the highest of all creation, can use the myriad things of the world to satisfy our daily needs through the labors of our own bodies and minds and, as long as we do not infringe upon the rights of others, may pass our days in happiness freely and independently. Nevertheless, as we broadly survey the human scene, there are the wise and the stupid, the rich and poor, the noble and lowly, whose conditions seem to differ as greatly as the clouds and the mud. Why is this? The reason is clear. In the *Jitsugo-kyō*† we read that if a man does not learn he will remain ignorant, and such an ignorant man is stupid. Therefore the question of the difference between wise and stupid is traceable to the degree of learning.

Again, there are difficult and easy professions in society. The person who performs difficult work is regarded as a man of high station whereas one who performs easy work is called a person of low station. Because work involving intellectual effort is considered more difficult than work done through one's own physical strength, such persons as doctors, scholars, government officials, merchants who manage large businesses,

---

† [*Jitsugo-kyō* was a textbook for children, completed in the Heian Period (from the late eighth to late twelfth centuries) and written in Chinese. From the Edo to the early Meiji Periods, it was widely published and used at *terakoya* (temple-schools) as well as at home.]

or farmers who employ many hands, are considered nobler and of higher station. Being such, their households naturally prosper, so that they seem to tower above and out of reach of the lower levels of society. But when we inquire into the reason for this, we find that these differences are entirely the result of whether they have or have not acquired the powers which learning brings. It is not because of some decree of Heaven. As the proverb says: Heaven does not give riches and dignity to the person himself, but to his labors. And so, as I said above, there are no innate status distinctions separating the noble and base, the rich and the poor. It is only the person who has studied diligently so as to have acquired a deep knowledge of things who becomes noble and rich, while his opposite becomes base and poor.

In essence, learning does not consist in such impractical pursuits as study of obscure Chinese characters, reading ancient texts which are difficult to make out, or enjoying and writing poetry. These kinds of learning may be useful diversions, but they should not be regarded as highly as the Confucian and Japanese Learning scholars have esteemed them since ancient times. Among the Confucian Learning scholars, those who have been skilled in practical matters have been few indeed. Rare also has been the *chōnin* (townsfolk) who, if he was well versed in poetry, was also successful in business. Consequently we still observe that thoughtful townsfolk and peasants, when they see their own children concentrating on books, fear as good parents that they will eventually bring the family fortune to ruin. This is not without reason. And it proves that such forms of learning are ultimately without practical value and will not serve daily needs.

Such impractical studies should be relegated to a secondary position. The object of one's primary efforts should be a practical learning that is closer to ordinary human needs. For example, a person should learn the 47-letter *kana* syllabary, methods of letter writing and of accounting, the practice of the abacus, the way to handle weights and measures, and the like. And there is much additional knowledge to be acquired. Geography is the guide to the climates not only of Japan, but of the many countries of the world. Physics is the science which investigates the properties and functions of the myriad things of the universe. History books chronicle in detail the conditions of the countries of the past and present.

Economics explains the financial management of self, family, and the state. Ethics expounds the natural principles of personal moral cultivation and of social intercourse. For the purpose of studying each of these areas, a person should investigate translations of Western books. In many cases he can use *kana*. But a lad who is young and talented in letters should be taught to read in the Western languages. By grasping the practical matters of each science, which vary in subject matter and content, he can search for the truth of things and make them serve his present purposes.

The above-mentioned subjects are ones common to mankind, matters which everyone should have an interest in, irrespective of rank or position. After acquiring learning in these areas, individuals can go on to do their duties or manage their family businesses, with independence redounding to the individuals, families, and the nation alike.

But in the pursuit of learning it is necessary that each person knows his capacity. We are born unrestricted and unbounded, and full-fledged men and women are free to act as they wish. Nevertheless, many will become selfish and fall into dissipation if they assert only their own freedom and do not know their place. "Place" or capacity means to achieve one's own personal freedom without infringing upon that of others, based on natural principle and in harmony with human feeling. The borderline between freedom and selfishness lies at the point where one does or does not infringe upon the freedom of others. For example, as far as a person spends his own money, it appears as if he can indulge in pleasures and dissipation to his heart's content. But this is hardly true: his dissipation becomes an example to others. In the long run, it will harm public morals and become an obstacle to public education. Therefore, even though such a dissolute person spends his own money, his offense is still reprehensible.

Again, freedom and independence refer not only to the private self, but to the nation as well. Japan is an island country separated eastward from the Asian continent. From ancient times it has not had relations with foreign countries. It has relied on its own products and has been self-sufficient. But foreign trade began after the coming of the Americans in the 1850s, creating the situation which has continued up to the present. Even after the opening of the ports there have been various debates. Some factions made a great deal of noise about "national seclusion" (*sakoku*) and "expulsion of the foreigners" (*jōi*). But their views were short-sighted. They were narrow-minded like the proverbial frog at the bottom of the well, and their arguments were not worth listening to. Japan and the nations of the West are peoples who live between the same heaven and earth, feel the warmth of the same sun, look up at the same moon, share the same oceans and air, and possess the same human feelings. Therefore, nations which have should share with those which have not. We should mutually teach and learn from each other, without shame or pride. We should promote each other's interests and pray for each other's happiness. We should associate with one another following the laws of Heaven and humanity. Such an attitude, based on reason, implies acknowledging one's guilt even before the black slaves of Africa; but it also means standing on principle without fear of the warships of England and America. It further implies that if this nation is disgraced, every Japanese citizen, to the last man, must sacrifice his life to prevent the decline of her prestige and glory. National independence entails all of these things.

By contrast, nations such as China has behaved as if there were no other countries in the world but their own. Whenever they see foreigners, they call them barbarians, and revile and scorn them as animals. Without calculating the power of their own country, they have recklessly attempted to banish the foreigners, only to be rebuked by the foreigners in return. Such a situation can be said to have come about because they did not truly understand the "place" of a single nation. If their case be compared to that of an individual person, they have been like someone who has fallen into selfish and dissolute habits because he has not attained natural freedom.

In our own case, since the Meiji Restoration the ways of the Japanese government have been greatly improved. In foreign affairs, we have regular relations with foreign nations in accord with international law. Internally, the government has promulgated the independence of the people, and has already allowed the use of family names and horse riding to the commoners. These changes are among the most commendable since the founding of the nation. It must be said that here the basis of social equality between the four former classes—samurai, farmers, artisans, and merchants—has finally been established. From the present day forward, there will be no such thing as hereditary class rank among the Japanese people. A man will have rank only by dint of his talents, virtues, and accomplishments.

As a case in point, while it is natural that we show deference to a government official, this is not because of the dignity of that person's status. He is accorded that respect only because he performs that important role through his talent and virtues, and because he deals with weighty laws for the sake of the people. It is the laws which have dignity, not the man. Everyone knows about the notorious processions of the shogun's tea vessels along the Tōkaidō† during the period of the Tokugawa shogunate; not only the tea vessels, even the shogun's hunting hawks had greater dignity than men. Travelers along the highway had to get off the road at the coming of the shogun's horses. Everything to which the shogun's use was attached, down to the stones and tiles, was invested with awe and dignity. While the people hated these things in their hearts since time immemorial, they naturally perpetuated these practices. Both high and low observed these terrible customs. In short, this was not because of the dignity of the laws or the intrinsic value of those things. It was because the government used craven methods to swell their prestige, and thereby to make men cower, and to prevent their freedom. They were false and vainglorious practices. Today such wretched institutions and customs have all been abolished throughout Japan. Therefore people should be relieved and if ever they harbor any feeling of injustice against the government, they will not have to swallow their resentment and hate the government in silence. They can seek out the office or authorities concerned, quietly lodge their complaints, and discuss them openly. If their case is in accord with natural principle and human feeling, they should not hesitate to fight for it even at the risk of their lives. These are now the "responsibility" of the citizens of the nation.

As indicated above, the principle of Heaven grants freedom from bondage to each individual person, and each individual country is free

---

† [The Tōkaidō (East-Sea Highway), which connected Kyoto and Edo (Tokyo), was one of the most important of the Five Highways in the Edo Period. Fukuzawa refers to the old practice of carrying tea with vessels for the shogun in Edo from Uji, a famous tea-growing region in Kyoto.]

from bondage as well. Consequently, if there is some threat which might infringe upon a country's freedom, that country should not hesitate to take up arms against all the countries of the world. Analogously, if there is someone infringing upon another person's individual freedom, the threatened party should not fear even the officials of the government. Now that in these times the basis of the equality of all classes of society has been established, each and every citizen can enjoy peace and do his own work to his own liking in accord with natural principle. On the other hand, since every person has his own individual "place," each person must also have the virtues and talents appropriate to it. It is necessary to know the principles of things in order to possess requisite talents and virtues. And it is necessary to study in order to know the principles of things. This, in short, is the reason for the urgency I have placed upon learning.

Surveying the developments of recent times, we see that the peasants, artisans, and merchants have risen in dignity a hundred times over their former social statuses, gradually reaching the point of standing on equal footing with the ex-samurai. Today even employment in government service is open to men of character and talent among the formerly non-samurai groups. Therefore they must be aware of their own personal dignity and place a high value on it, not acting in a base manner. But again, there are no individuals more pitiable and despicable than the ignorant and illiterate. The height of ignorance is to be shameless. When such people, through their own ignorance, have fallen into poverty and are hard pressed by hunger and cold, they recklessly hate the rich around them instead of blaming their own stupidity. In the extreme, they form cliques and mount rebellion and insurrection to press their demands. Such solutions can be said to be shameless as well as law-defying. If people who relied on the laws of the realm to preserve their own security and to conduct their own businesses were to follow only those laws which suited their purposes while breaking those which did not accord with their selfish ends, would not the former and latter practices be contradictory? In addition, there are cases of people secure in fortune and from respectable families who know how to amass wealth, but do not know how to educate properly their own children. Since their young have not been properly educated, it is no wonder that they are ignorant. They gradually sink into idleness and dissipation, and there are not a few who in short order ruin the family estate of their ancestors.

The method of rational persuasion is useless to control such stupid people. The government is forced to use power to intimidate them. It is because of this that a Western proverb says that there must be a harsh government over stupid people. It is not that the government is harsh; the stupid people have invited this misfortune upon themselves. Conversely, it is reasonable that there should be good government over good people. Therefore in Japan, too, we will have this kind of government if the people are this way. If the morality of the people sinks below its present level and ignorance and illiteracy increase, then the laws of the government must correspondingly become harsher. Conversely, if the people pursue learning, understand the principles of things, and follow the way of modern civilization, then the laws of the government will also become more generous and compassionate. The severity or leniency of the law will naturally be in proportion to the virtue of the people. Who would cherish a harsh government, and dislike a good one? Who would not pray for the wealth and prestige of his own nation? Who would tolerate the contempt of foreign nations? These are ordinary feelings of human nature.

One who is patriotic of mind in contemporary society should not be anxious to the extent of disturbing his body and soul. His important aims should be as follows: to let each person conduct himself correctly on the basis of human nature, then diligently pursue learning and broaden his knowledge, and thirdly possess knowledge and virtue appropriate to his station in life. Both government and people should have the common purpose that each function in its proper capacity, so that the peace of the country can be maintained, the government smoothly administering the affairs of the state, and the people not suffering under its rule. The learning which I am now exhorting has this sole end in view.

POSTSCRIPT

On the occasion of the opening of a school in my old town of Nakatsu,

I wrote this piece encouraging learning to present to some old friends there. One of them persuaded me that it would be of greater benefit if I published it widely instead of just circulating it among my old friends in Nakatsu. I have therefore printed it at the Keio-gijuku to make my thoughts known to my colleagues.

February 1871

Fukuzawa Yukichi
Obata Tokujirō

Section
TWO

FOREWORD

LEARNING in the broad sense can be divided into immaterial and material spheres. The former includes such subjects as ethics (*shingaku*), theology, and metaphysics; the latter, astronomy, geography, physics, and chemistry. Each branch of learning broadens the range of our knowledge and experience, gives us discernment into the principles of things and understanding of our duties as persons. In order to widen our knowledge and experience, we must hear what others have to say, form our own ideas, and read books as well. Accordingly, although it is essential to know letters to study, it would be a great misunderstanding of the nature of learning to think that it only consists in reading books, as people have thought from ancient times. Letters are the instruments of learning; they are like the hammers and saws used to build a house. Although hammers and saws are indispensable tools for building a house, a person who only knows their names but not how to build a house cannot be called a carpenter. For this reason, a person who only knows how to read letters but does not know how to discern the principles of things cannot be called a true scholar. Such a person is like a man who is said to have read the Confucian *Analects* but does not understand it. In like manner, a person who has learned to recite the *Kojiki*† by heart but does not know the present price of rice must be

---

† [The *Kojiki* (Record of Ancient Matters) is Japan's earliest extant written record, compiled in 712 A.D., and containing tales of the gods and accounts of Japan's earliest history. It was one of the major texts of the National Learning school.]

called ignorant in practical studies. A person who has mastered the inner meaning of the Chinese Classics and Histories but does not understand the ways of buying and selling, and is quite incompetent in business dealings, must be said to be a failure in the art of book-keeping. And a person who, after years of hard study and huge outlays of money, becomes proficient in Western studies but is unable to make his own private living, is out of touch with learning pertinent to the current of the times. Such people may be called mere wholesalers of letters. In merit and capacity they are not different from food-consuming dictionaries. They are useless to the nation, and parasites on the economy. Therefore, household management, book-keeping, staying abreast of the trends of the times are also forms of learning. What is the reason for understanding learning exclusively in the sense of reading Japanese, Chinese, and Western books? I have entitled this book *An Encouragement of Learning*, but I am hardly advocating an exclusive study of books.

In this work, I have expressed the general meaning of learning, sometimes by quoting literally and sometimes by paraphrasing Western sources, as well as by citing matters which should be known by everyone in respect to both material and immaterial spheres of learning. As a follow-up to the previous section, I will broaden this theme here, and continue with it in the third and fourth sections as well.

THE EQUALITY OF MEN

At the beginning of the first section I declared that all men are equal, and that they can live in freedom and independence without hereditary status distinctions. Let me further develop that idea here. The birth of man is the work of nature and not the power of man. People should love and respect one another, and each person should fullfil his own duty without infringing upon others. For they are persons of the same species who share the same heaven and are creatures between the same heaven and earth. Thus, for example, the reason that brothers in the same household should cherish one another is that they are children of the same family, and have the same parents whom they serve. This relationship has been enunciated as a great ethical principle.

And similarly, if I inquire into the balance of human relations, I must again say that all men are equal. However, they may not be equal in outward appearances. Equality means equality in essential human rights, even though in external conditions there may be extreme differences between rich and poor, strong and weak, intelligent and stupid persons. Some nobles descended from feudal lords still live in palaces, dress in luxurious clothing, and eat sumptuous foods; there are others who rent their lodgings in back alleys and hardly eke out a living from day to day. Some become the public officials and merchants who move the world with their splendid talents and knowledge; others, without wisdom and discernment, spend their lives as candy vendors. Some become powerful sumo wrestlers; others, delicate princesses. But while they differ like the clouds above and the mud below, still, from the point of view of inherent human rights, all men are equal without the least distinction among them.

In other terms, human rights are the great moral obligations that give dignity to an individual human life, protect a man's fortune and possessions, and dignify his honor and reputation. When Heaven gives birth to man, it gives him faculties of body and mind and the powers to realize his rights in practice. Therefore under no circumstances should a man be deprived of his rights. The lives of the feudal lord and laborers were equal in essential value. A rich merchant protects his million *ryō* no more than the candy vendor protects his four *mon*, each as his own personal property. A proverb about the ills of society says: "It is impossible to deal with crying children or the lord of a manor." Another says: "Parents and masters make unreasonable requests." As these proverbs suggest, there are persons who think that human rights can be twisted. But this is a misunderstanding and confusion of the outward appearances of things with essential human rights. The estate steward and his peasants may have differed in outward circumstances, but they were equal in essential human rights. What was distressing for the peasants was also distressing for the steward; what was sweet for the steward was also sweet for the peasants. It is human nature to avoid what is distressing and to take the sweet. And it is a basic human right for a person to be able to attain what he wants, as long as he does not infringe upon the rights of others. There was not the slightest distinction between the rights of a steward and his peasants. It was just that the steward was powerful and wealthy, the peasants weak and poor. Wealth and power are relative conditions of man, and of course they are different. But if today one man acts unjustly toward a weak and poor person through his wealth and power, is this not a violation of the other's rights by taking advantage that their external circumstances are unequal? It would be comparable to a strong-armed sumo wrestler breaking the arm of his neighbor. His neighbor is of course weaker, but even though weaker he can still use his arm to accomplish his own purposes. Therefore it would be an outrageous infringement if the weaker man's arm were broken by the wrestler for no good reason at all.

Let me now extend the above argument to the matters of society. In the time of the Tokugawa shogunate, the distinction between samurai and common people was sharply drawn. The military families recklessly brandished their prestige. They treated the peasants and townsfolk as despicable criminals. They enacted such notorious laws as that which gave a samurai the right to cut down a commoner. According to these laws the lives of the commoners were not truly their own, but merely borrowed things. The peasants and merchants had to prostrate themselves before the samurai, although they had no connection with them. On the roads they had to give way to them, and indoors to yield their mats to them. In the extreme case, they suffered the outrage of not being allowed to ride the horses they had reared in their own stables.

The above abuses were instances of injustice between the samurai and commoners in individual relations. But when it comes to the relation between government and people, matters were even worse. Not only the shogunate, but the 300 daimyo each presided over small-scale governments in their individual domains. They treated the common peasants and townsfolk despotically. They sometimes seemed compassionate to them, but they did not really recognize their inherent human rights. And there were many reprehensible practices. However, as I have declared above, the feudal governments and the people differed only in their relative strength; there was no difference in inherent human rights. The peasants grew rice to feed the people. The townsfolk engaged in buying and selling goods for the convenience of society. These were the businesses of peasants and merchants, respectively. The government established laws, by which it controlled the wicked and protected the good; and this was the business of the government. This government's business cost a great deal of money; since it had neither rice nor cash to meet its expenses, it entered into an agreement with the commoners that the latter should pay taxes in rice and money to fund its treasury. This was the contract, in other words, between government and people. Therefore the peasants and townsfolk could fullfil their duties by paying taxes and obeying the laws, while the government fulfilled its duties by taking these taxes to make due payments for its expenses and to protect the people. As long as both sides fulfilled their obligations without violating this contract, there could be no further objections; and thus each side was freely implementing its rights.

However, in the time of the Tokugawa shogunate, the government was called *ue-sama*.† Those who went on official missions could recklessly brandish their prestige. Not only that, they would eat at the inns along their way without paying. They did not pay their fares for river crossings, and did not pay their carriers' wages. The worst extreme was extorting money from their carriers to spend for drinking sake. These were outrageous cases of "Might makes right"—as when, to suit a personal whim, a feudal lord would build a house or undertake some needless enterprise through the good offices of some government official, thus squandering money uselessly. When he ran short of funds, he would increase the land-tax levies or collect incidental taxes and make some high-sounding declaration that he was repaying his indebtedness to the country.

But what did this indebtedness to the country mean? Presumably it meant that the peasants and townsfolk could continue to work in peace and live without fear of robbery or murder because of the government's protection; however, it was already the business and proper duty of the government to make laws and protect the people. Therefore it could not properly be called kindness on the government's part. If the government thought that it was acting out of kindness, then the peasants and townsmen could also have said that, for their part, their tax payments

---

† [This is one of the honorifics used when addressing people of noble and high rank, such as emperor, shogun, or daimyo. *Ue* literally means "above" and "high" and *sama* is a suffix normally attached to names in order to show politeness.]

were also acts of kindness. If the government regarded the lawsuits of the people as its burden, then the people could also have said that it was burdensome to give up five out of every ten straw bags of their rice crop for land taxes. Thus the matter could be haggled about endlessly. At any rate, if there was indebtedness on both sides, it did not stand to reason that one side should have to express its gratitude unilaterally.

When we inquire into the cause of such evil customs, we find that the government had violated the great principle of the equality of man by taking advantage of the conditions of wealth and poverty, strength and weakness, as evil instruments to obstruct the rights of the poor through its own wealth and power. Therefore we must keep uppermost in mind that all men are inherently equal. This is the most important principle of human society. It is called **reciprocity** or **equality** in the West. This is what I referred to, in the beginning of Section One, as the equality of all men. In the present argument, I champion the side of the peasants and townsfolk to strengthen their position as much as possible. But there is also an argument on the other side. Generally speaking, in dealing with the people, harshness or moderation in the law must be proportionate to the nature of the people. The essential relation between people and government is that they constitute one entity, with distinctions only in functions and duties. There is a strict covenant that the government should act as deputy and lawmaker for the people, while the people should obey the laws without fail.

Thus for example the people of the present Meiji Period have contracted with the present government to obey its laws. Therefore, once the laws have been established, they cannot be changed before their revision, even if they inconvenience some individuals. They must be conscientiously and respectfully observed, for that is precisely the duty of the people. But there are some ignorant and illiterate persons who do not know the principles of right and wrong. Their only talents are those of eating, sleeping, and rising. They are ignorant, but they are also greedy. They cheat people right before their eyes and skillfully evade the laws of the government. They know neither the laws of the nation nor their own duties. They have many children, but they do not know how to educate them. They are shameless and lawless fools. If the descendants of such people flourish, they will not benefit the country.

On the contrary, there may be some who bring it positive harm. It is quite impossible to use reason in dealing with such stupid people. Even though it is against our will, there is no other expediency than to intimidate them with force so as to prevent greater harm. This is one reason why there have been tyrannical governments in the world. Such indeed was the situation not only of the shogunate in Japan but also of the countries of Asia since ancient times. Accordingly a nation's harsh government is not necessarily attributable to a tyrant or tyrannical officials. The people, through their own ignorance, bring down such misfortune upon themselves. There have been some who, instigated by others, have plotted assassinations, or who, misunderstanding the new laws, have risen up in revolt. Others, in the name of pressing their claims for justice, have broken into the houses of the rich, have drunk their sake, and have robbed them of their money. Their "solutions" can scarcely be called human. Even Buddha or Confucius could not devise measures to deal with such burglars. Eventually, the law has to be harshly applied. And consequently I am saying that if people want to avoid tyrannical government, they must forthwith set their mind to the pursuit of learning, so as to elevate their own talents and virtues to a position of equality with the government. This is precisely the purport of the learning I am encouraging.

Section
THREE

THE EQUALITY OF NATIONS

In the previous section I stated that all men, whether rich or poor, strong or weak, members of the government or citizens of the government, have the same inherent human rights (*kengi*).* Here I want to broaden its meaning to discuss the relations between nations as well. Since a nation is a society of people, Japan is a society of the Japanese, England of the English. Japanese and English both live between the same heaven and the same earth. Therefore there is no reason why they should infringe upon each other's rights. If there is no reason for one man to harm another, there is equally no reason for two men to harm two others. The same principle applies for one million or ten million; the truth of things does not change according to the number of persons involved.

Now in surveying the present world scene, we find that there are strong and wealthy nations which may be called civilized and enlightened and in which learning and the arts of war are highly developed. There are also poor and weak nations which are barbarous or savage and in which culture and military capacities are still low.† In general, the

---

* I will hereafter shorten the phrase *kenri tsūgi*, employed in Section Two, to *kengi*. Both terms correspond to the English word **rights**.

† [Fukuzawa also introduces this idea of Western Enlightenment that all societies progress through stages as the "ages of civilization" in his *An Outline of a Theory of Civilization* (1875). He divides civilization's development into three phases—the primitive stage, the semi-developed stage, and civilization—and he places Japan in the semi-developed stage.]

nations of Europe and America illustrate the first category, those of Asia and Africa the second. Nevertheless, the wealth and strength of nations are outward appearances, and it is natural that they are all different. But if the strong and wealthy powers oppress the poor and weak nations, it would be no different from the sumo wrestler in my previous example who could break the arm of a sick person. By reason of the inherent rights of nations, this cannot be allowed. Modern-day Japan as well cannot compare in wealth and strength with the nations of the West; but by reason of the inherent rights of nations, Japan is not the least inferior. If the day comes when Japan suffers injustice from without, we should not fear to take on the whole world as our enemy.

As I have said above in the first section, this is the case in which every Japanese citizen, to the last man, should be willing to sacrifice his life to prevent the decline of the prestige and glory of Japan. Moreover, the outward circumstances of national wealth and power are not irrevocably fixed by nature's decree. They can be changed by the diligent efforts of men. Today's fools can become tomorrow's sages. The rich and mighty of the past can become the poor and weak today. There are not a few examples of this in both ancient and modern times. If we Japanese begin to pursue learning with spirit and energy, so as to achieve personal independence and thereby enrich and strengthen the nation, why should we fear the Powers of the West? Let us associate with men of truth, and be rid of those who are not. In a nutshell, national independence must follow from personal independence.

NATIONAL INDEPENDENCE THROUGH PERSONAL INDEPENDENCE

As I have just said, all nations are equal; but when the people of a nation do not have the spirit of individual independence, the corresponding right of national independence cannot be realized. There are three reasons for this, which I shall develop below.

I persons without the spirit of personal independence will not have deep concern for their country.

Independence means to manage one's own personal affairs and not to have a mind to depend upon others. The person who can himself discern the right and wrong of things, and who does not err in the measures he takes, is independent of the wisdom of others. The person who makes his own livelihood through his own physical or mental labors is independent of the financial support of others. If people do not have these independent qualities of mind and are merely reliant on the power of others, the entire nation will be dependents and there will be no one to support them. It will be like a procession of blind men without a guide. Would this not be absurd? Some may say that "the people should be kept in a state of dependence and left uninformed" [*Analects*]; or that for every thousand blind men there are equally a thousand with sight. Thus, they say, let the wise control the masses from above; let the masses obey the will of their superiors from below. This argument is in fact from the school of Confucius. But it is a great error in actual fact. And in fact there is only one in a thousand who possesses sufficient talent and virtue to be able to govern others in the nation.

Let us suppose that there is a country of a million citizens, of which a thousand are wise, and the more than 999,000 are ignorant. Suppose that the great majority could be controlled by the talent and virtue of the wise minority, who would love them as children or tend them as sheep. They could, by both kind and severe measures, show them the direction the government is to take. The result might be that the masses would unconsciously obey the orders of their superiors. There would be no incidents of robbery and murder, and there would be peace and good government throughout the land. But essentially this is not the case. This hypothetical nation's people are divided into masters and guests. The masters are the one thousand intelligent persons who direct the affairs of the state. The rest are ignorant guests. Being only guests, they have few real concerns. They rely entirely on their masters without taking any initiative themselves. Therefore their solicitude for their country will not be as great as their masters'. Their attitude will indeed be like that of strangers. As long as we are talking about the internal affairs of the nation, they may be bypassed. But if war should break out with a foreign country, the absurdity of this arrangement will become clear. The ignorant and powerless masses may not betray their country, but there will be many who will desert the cause, saying that "since we are only guests, sacrificing our lives is uncalled for." Thus the population of the country is nominally a million strong, but when it comes to defending the nation is considerably less in actual count. It would be quite impossible for such a nation to maintain its independence.

As I have said above, Japan must be filled with the spirit of independence if we are to defend her against foreign threats. Every citizen must take the responsibility of the nation upon himself, regardless of personal status or prestige. Both the learned and the ignorant, the blind and those who have sight, must fulfill their obligations as citizens of the country. Englishmen should consider England to be their native soil; we Japanese should consider Japan to be ours. Since it is ours, we should treat our own native soil as our own homes. We should not hesitate to lose not only our fortunes but even our lives for the sake of our homeland. This is precisely the great duty of patriotism. Of course, the administration is the government, and those who are politically subordinate are the people. But this is only a division of roles for the sake of efficiency. When the honor of the whole nation is at stake, is it right for the duty of the citizens to be that of passive bystanders who delegate the affairs of state entirely to the government? Because the name of a country is used in the title of a person's name, as Mr. So-and-so of England, or Mr. So-and-so of Japan, each person has the right to pursue his daily life in freedom within that country. Once he has this right, he has its duties as well.

In the Sengoku Period [1467–1568], when Imagawa Yoshimoto of Suruga led an army of several tens of thousands against Oda Nobunaga, he was ambushed by Nobunaga at Okehazama.† Nobunaga then routed Yoshimoto's headquarters and beheaded him. The army of Suruga scattered like frightened spiders. They fled without a clash of

---

† [Fukuzawa is referring to the Battle of Okehazama in 1560. Oda Nobunaga (1534–82) defeated Imagawa Yoshimoto (1519–60), the military governor of Suruga, despite Imagawa's considerably larger forces. This victory at Okehazama marked the establishment of Oda Nobunaga as a powerful daimyo.]

arms. The then prestigious government of Imagawa of Suruga collapsed in a day and disappeared forever. Two or three years ago, the French emperor Napoleon III was captured by Prussia at the outbreak of the Franco-Prussian war. But the French not only did not abandon hope, they fought back with even greater spirits. They fought with their very blood and guts. After holding firm for several months, a treaty was finally signed, and France had survived. Her fate was entirely different from that of Imagawa. What is the reason for this difference? It is because the people of Suruga were entirely dependent upon Yoshimoto alone. Their status was that of guests who did not regard Suruga as their own native province. In France there were many patriotic citizens, each of whom took the responsibility of the nation's crisis upon himself and fought for his own land without needing to be persuaded by others. This made the difference between ancient Suruga and modern France. Judging from this case, we can infer how, in a crisis calling for national defense, those who have the spirit of independence will exhibit deep concern for their country, in contrast to those who have not.

II those without the spirit of independence within themselves will also be unable to exercise their right of independence when in contact with foreigners outside.

Those who lack the spirit of independence necessarily rely on others. Those who rely on others fear them. Standing in fear of others, they must fawn upon them. Their fear and subordination gradually become habitual; they come to wear faces of brass. They know no shame, and do not speak out on questions which call for discussion. In confrontation with others, they only know how to bow to the waist. When this becomes habitual nature, it is not easily changed. For example, family names and horse riding have now been permitted the common people, and the law courts have modernized their ways. Therefore the official status of the commoners is equal to that of the ex-samurai families. Yet their old habits are not changing with equal rapidity. Their basic nature as commoners remains the same as in the days of old. Their speech and dealings with others are still those of inferiors. They cannot utter a single coherent phrase before superiors.

When told to stand, they stand; when told to dance, they dance. Their subservience is like that of hungry dogs raised in a house. They truly are spiritless and powerless with faces of brass.

In the ancient period of national seclusion under the rigid administration of the Tokugawa shogunate, the people were already spiritless. Not only did this not interfere with government practices, it was in fact advantageous. The shogunate purposely perpetuated their ignorance and subservience—indeed, the officials took pride in doing so. But now that Japan has formal relations with foreign nations, the lingering harm from such a policy is evident. For example, if a merchant from a rural area plucks up enough courage to dare to engage in trade with the foreigners at Yokohama, he will first be frightened at their physical size, then at the amounts of their money, the size of their trading houses, the speed of their steamships. He may utterly lose heart. If in the course of time he comes forward to do business with them, he will be boggled by their business techniques. When the foreigners press some unreasonable negotiation, he will not only be dazzled, but will shudder at their power and prestige. While he knows that their demands are unreasonable, he will end up taking huge losses as well as suffering great personal humiliation.

However, this will be the loss not only of that person, but of the entire nation; it will be the humiliation not only of a single individual, but also of Japan. This absurd spirit of the townsmen is the result of the fact that they have, for generation after generation, not tasted the spirit of independence. They have suffered under the samurai and been abused by the law courts. Even when they met with an *ashigaru* [footsoldier] who earned a minimum kind of feudal stipend, the townsmen had to look up to him as a superior. This subservient spirit permeated the very marrow of their bones; it could not be washed away overnight. Thus it is not unreasonable that such cowardly people should lose heart before the bold and intrepid foreigners. And their conduct demonstrates my contention that those who lack personal independence cannot stand up independently before foreigners.

III those who lack the spirit of independence rely on the power of others and sometimes perpetrate evil deeds.

In the time of the Tokugawa shogunate there were some persons who used the name of prestigious daimyo such as the *Sanke*† to lend money with which they engaged in very unjust transactions. Their manipulations were extremely detestable. If someone was not paid back borrowed money, he should have spared no efforts in making repeated appeals to the courts. But if he dared not appeal out of fear of the government, was it not even more cowardly for him to demand his money back by threatening with the name and power of others? We no longer hear of such incidents, but are there not some who are now availing themselves of the prestige of foreigners? I do not yet have clear evidence of this, and so I cannot state it positively. But considering past practices, I am not without my suspicions about such dealings in present-day society as well. Hereafter, if there is any case of mixed residence with foreigners in which someone uses their reputation to do evil, it will indeed be an indescribable curse upon the nation. Therefore let us not relax our vigilance, saying that it is easy to deal with people who have no spirit of independence. Calamity can arise from unexpected quarters. The weaker the spirit of independence in the people, the stronger will be the danger of the nation being betrayed. This is precisely an instance of perpetrating evil by relying on others, of which I spoke above.

I have enumerated above three instances of misfortune to the nation caused by the absence of the spirit of independence in the people. If there are persons who have the spirit of patriotism to any degree, they must now plan to cultivate their own personal independence, without regard to whether they belong to the public or private sectors of society. If they have enough strength, they must also assist others to achieve their own independence. Parents and elder brothers should foster it in their children and younger brothers; teachers should encourage it in their pupils. No matter what social origins, every man must stand up independently and protect Japan. In short, a common liberation of man and a common share of the

---

† [*Sanke*, the "three Houses" connected with the Tokugawa: namely, the families of the daimyo of Kii, Mito, and Owari, which were eligible to provide an heir of the shogun.]

nation's joys and sorrows will be better than the initiative of the few who bind the majority to their will and bear the burdens of government alone.

Section
FOUR

THE DUTY OF SCHOLARS

Listen quietly to what intelligent people are saying these days. Some raise the questions of whether Japan—whose future fate of course cannot be known—might be in danger of losing her independence, or will gradually progress to a high level of prosperity and civilization by keeping stride with the force of events, as she is now actually doing. Others are more skeptical. They feel we should reserve judgment concerning Japanese independence for two or three decades. Still others make the criticism that if we follow the advice of some foreigners who actually despise Japan, our national independence will be greatly endangered. Needless to say, these are only opinions; they do not immediately coerce our belief or weaken our self-confidence. But these attitudes towards Japanese independence must have some basis in fact, or they would not be consciously entertained.

Suppose that we now go to England and ask if British independence is in doubt. People will laugh; and indeed, why is it that no one doubts? For British independence is beyond the realm of doubt. This is quite different from our own case. Japanese civilization may seem to have advanced in certain respects over its past conditions, but in the final analysis we still cannot avoid raising this question of Japan's independence in the modern world. Should not every native Japanese citizen be concerned about this state of affairs? I myself am a native Japanese. Already being Japanese, I, like every other, should understand and perform my duty. Of course, public administration is the duty of the government, but in human affairs there are also many areas in which the government should not get involved. Therefore, people and government must each contribute their share to the public good. We must perform our duty as people, and the government its duty as the government, each assisting the other to preserve national independence.

There must be a balance of power to maintain any system. For example, in order to maintain physical health, food, air, and sunlight are all necessary components. We respond internally to external stimuli such as cold, heat, pain, itching; in this way we harmonize our bodily movements. If the external stimuli were suddenly withdrawn and the body was left to its internal processes only, our physical health would not last a single day.

The same principle obtains with a nation of people. The government is a country's internal processes. Their harmonious functioning for the maintenance of national independence requires a balance of internal governmental power with the external power of its people. The government is the body and the people are its outside stimuli. Our national independence would also not last a single day were the external stimuli removed and the government left with only its own inner organs. A person who understands the structure of the human body and can see the analogy with a country's economic system will have no doubts about my comparison.

Judging from Japan's present situation, we have not yet reached the level of the West in the areas of scholarship, business, and law. But modern civilization is chiefly built upon the foundation of these three areas of endeavor. Without sufficient progress in these three areas, a nation's independence can clearly not be maintained. In Japan, however, not one of these spheres has reached maturity.

Since the Meiji Restoration, talented men in government offices have devoted their considerable abilities to national problems. But because of certain unavoidable obstacles in their path, progress has been slower than expected. The chief obstacles have been the ignorance and illiteracy of the people. The government well understands what these obstacles are, and is accordingly promoting learning, clarifying the law, and instructing the people in ways to engage in business enterprises. It has both given advice to the people and taken the initiative itself in certain enterprises. Still, while it has been trying all possible means, the results have not been successful up to now. In fact, the government is as despotic as before, and the Japanese people continue to be stupid, spiritless and powerless. The slight progress made is out of all proportion to the energies and money spent for it. Why is this? In the last analysis, it is because the civilization of a nation cannot be made to advance solely through the power of the government.

Some people are saying that it is only a temporary expediency to use governmental means to manage the stupid people until they have sufficiently developed their intellectual and moral levels to be able to enter the stage of modern civilization on their own. This theory is easy to enunciate but difficult to realize in practice. Since time immemorial, the people of the whole country have suffered under despotic rule which did not allow freedom of expression. They stole security by deception, and escaped punishment by telling lies. Fraud and subterfuge became necessary tools of life; injustice and insincerity became daily routine. No one felt ashamed and no one asked questions. Honor fell to the ground and disappeared with the wind of the times. How, then, did men have time to love their country? Trying to correct these evil tendencies, the government would brandish its false authority all the more to intimidate and reprove them. But forcing them to be sincere only had the contrary effect. The situation was like using fire to extinguish fire. In the end, the superior and inferior strata of society had grown further and further apart to form separate spiritual mind-sets.

These mind-sets (or so-called **spirits**) resist sudden change. In recent times, the external form of government has been overhauled, but its despotic and oppressive spirit continues as of old. The common people also retain their base and insincere spirit, even after acquiring their rights to some degree. This spirit is intangible, but quickly permeates an individual person. It is not describable from superficial observation, but its real effects are very strong. The truth of my argument can be seen in all forms of life today.

Let me give one example. There are not a few men of talent in government posts today. As I privately listen to what they have to say and observe their actions, I find they are all generally broadminded and magnanimous gentlemen; I not only cannot criticize them, but think that the speeches and conduct of some of them are admirable. From another point of view, even the commoners are not all foolish, spiritless, and powerless. There are some rare individuals who are just and sincere. But as I look at the actual accomplishments of these gentlemen in their government offices, I am disturbed at the way they administer the affairs of state. In addition, the good and faithful common people, as soon as they come in contact with the government, are prone shamelessly to abandon their principles in order to deceive the officials with fraud and tricks. Why is it that such mediocrity and baseness are the order of the day? It is as if they had a body with two heads. In private life they are wise; in office, stupid. If dispersed, there is light; when gathered, darkness. I might say that the government is an institution wherein the wisdom of the many gathers to conduct the affairs of foolish people. This is indeed an absurd state of affairs.

In short, the reason might lie in the fact that, having been oppressed by this spirit, the people have not been able to exercise their natural abilities to the full. Since the Meiji Restoration, the government has been trying to promote scholarship, law, and commerce, but without much result, for the same reason. But now, should the government control the people through a temporary expediency until their intellectual and moral capacities develop to an adequate level, and thus coerce the people to become civilized? Or if not that, must it devise a way to deceive them to be good? If the government imposes its authority, the people will respond with falsehood; and if the government uses fraud, the people will only superficially obey. This cannot be called the best policy. Even if it were skillfully executed, it would be of no real benefit to the advancement of civilization. I conclude therefore that Japan's civilization cannot be made to progress solely by use of government power.

In consideration of the above, I hold that Japanese civilization will advance only after we sweep away the old spirit that permeates the minds of the people. But it can be swept away by neither government decree nor private admonition. Some persons must take the initiative in practice to show the people where their aims should lie. We cannot look to the farmers, the merchants, or scholars of Japanese or Chinese Learning to personify these aims. It is rather only the scholars of Western Learning who must fill this role. But they are not entirely measuring up to this assignment. Their numbers have increased of late, and they are giving instructions in Western texts or reading translations. They seem to be expending every effort, but in fact there are not a few about whose doings I have some misgivings. Many are merely reading the words without understanding, or, while understanding they do not have the sincerity to put the meanings into practice. I have more than a few doubts about their actual behavior: such scholars and gentlemen are aware of the existence of official posts but unaware of the existence of their private selves; they know how to stand above the government but not how to be under it. They have ultimately not been able to shake off the bad habits of the scholars of Chinese Learning. They have Chinese bodies dressed up in Western clothes.

Let me give actual proof. At the present time, most of this kind of scholars of Western Learning have entered government service. I can easily count on my fingers only a few of them who engage in the private sector. The reason for this trend is that the former are greedy for profit and desire to fulfill their long-cherished ambitions for fame. But the reason for this trend can never be ascribed to their greed for profit alone; because of their ingrained education, they have had the sole desire of becoming government officials, being obsessed with the idea that nothing can be achieved except through the government. Even persons of high authority and reputation fall under this category of scholar-officials. Their conduct appears to be slavish; their intentions, however, are not always bad: it is just that because they have become intoxicated with the spirit of society, they are unaware how contemptible their conduct actually is. This holds true for even scholars of great reputation. How, then, can the people at large fail to imitate them? If a young student reads only a few volumes, he immediately aspires for a post in the government. Young and ambitious merchants want to do business in the name of the government as soon as they have a few hundred gold coins for capital. Schools are licensed by the government, as are preaching, cattle grazing, and sericulture. Almost seventy to eighty per cent of private enterprises have some government connection. Therefore the minds of the people bend more and more to government ways. They admire and trust, or fear and flatter, the government officials. No one has the sincerity of mind to be independent. Their disgraceful conduct is hardly endurable.

Newspapers being published at the present time, as well as certain written memorials, also illustrate this trend. Though regulations for publication are not very strict, the newspapers never carry opinions unfavorable to the authorities. To the contrary, every commendable trifle about the government is praised in bold letters. They are like courtesans flattering their guests. If we read the memorials, we find that their wordings are always extremely base. They look up to the government as if it were some god. They look down upon themselves as if they were criminals. They use empty phrases which are unworthy of equal human beings. Yet no one thinks it shameful. From their writings alone we might surmise that these people were all madmen. Yet the publishers of these newspapers and the writers of these memorials are almost all scholars of Western Learning. In private life they are not necessarily courtesans or lunatics. Their extremes of insincerity are the result of the fact that, never having had an example of equal rights, they are oppressed and blindly led by the spirit of subservience. Thus they are not able to realize their real capacity as citizens. It is generally correct to say that in Japan there is only a government, and as yet no people. My conclusion is that the present crop of scholars of Western Learning cannot lead us in eliminating the old spirit of the people and in advancing Japanese civilization.

If my above argument be allowed, the government cannot be taken as the sole beneficiary of promoting civilization and maintaining national independence. Nor are we to rely on the scholars of Western Learning. Therefore I feel I can take it upon myself to lead the way for both the foolish Japanese people and for those Western scholars. As for myself, my own learning is of course inadequate, but I have long been involved in Western studies, and I am above the middle class in present-day Japan. As for the recent reforms in society, if I did not chiefly initiate them, I think I may have been indirectly influential in bringing them about. Even if my influence has been slight, I am satisfied with the reforms, and I am certain that people will also consider me something of a reformer. As I already have the name of a reformer, and occupy a position above the middle class, there may be some who will regard my doings as their model. If this is so, it should be my responsibility now to lead the way for the people.

Now, to accomplish anything at all, it is better to persuade than to command; and it is better to give personal example than to persuade. While this is true, the government has only the power of commanding; persuasion and actual example belong to the private sector. Therefore let me first exercise my private enterprise to lecture on the art of learning, go into business, discuss the law, write books, publish papers, etc. Let me do any or all of these things within the limits of my capacities and without offending others. Let me correctly manage my own affairs within the bounds of the law. Should I suffer injustice due to bad government decrees, I should exhort the government severely without subservience. For it is the extreme urgency of today to make the government wake up to the need of sweeping out old abuses and to revive the rights of the people.

Of course, private enterprises are complicated things, and persons who are involved in them may also have their good points. Therefore, it is not right that only a few scholars should take care of the whole undertaking. But I am hardly just trying to trumpet my own skill in meeting these challenges. I am rather trying to point out the direction of private initiatives. But one actual example is better than a hundred arguments. That is why I am giving the example of my own private work. My point is that human affairs should not merely be under government control. Scholars and townsfolk also have their own roles to play. The government is what it is, a Japanese government; and the people are what they are, the Japanese people. Therefore the people should be shown that they can approach the government without fear and suspicion. As they then come gradually to understand their goal, the ingrained spirits of both the despotism of the government and the social subservience of the people will gradually disappear. For the first time a Japanese people will be born who will be a stimulus to the government instead of its plaything. Scholarship, business, and law will naturally return to their rightful owners. There will be a balance of powers between government and the people, through which we shall be able to preserve national independence as well.

In summary, I have discussed the merits and demerits of scholars today becoming officials or remaining in the private sector to promote the independence of Japan, and this book sides with the latter position. To state things in general, what is not advantageous is necessarily harmful, and what is not profitable is necessarily a loss; there is nothing which is half profitable and half harmful. I am not advocating the private sector for my own gain. I am only discussing it on the basis of my own daily experience. If others can reject my position with strong evidence, or if they can clearly state the disadvantages of the private sector, I shall gladly defer to them. For my ultimate interest is the nation's welfare.

APPENDIX

There have been several objections to my main argument which I shall report here. The first states that there is no more convenient method than a strong government to get things done. To this I answer that we cannot solely rely on government power to promote civilization. This should already be clear from the main text. Moreover, despite its years of experience, the actual accomplishments of the government have not been so many. The private sector may also fail in the long run, but since there are clearly things to be said for it in theory, it should be given a try in practice. Those who doubt its efficacy without giving it a fair trial are not courageous men.

The second objection is that there are few talented men in the government, and if the government is impoverished of its personnel by these men leaving office for the private sector, this will be an embarrassment to the affairs of the government. To this I answer that the reverse is true. Today's government labors under the burden of too many officials. Reduction of the numbers of office holders by means of simplification of the work will have a twofold effect. Offices will be streamlined, and the retired personnel can meet other needs of society.

Indeed, the practice of multiplying offices and of using talented men in useless posts may be said to be a stupid policy. If these talented people leave public office, it will not be that they will leave Japan for foreign shores. They will still be contributing to Japan within Japan. Therefore this fear is ungrounded.

The third objection is that if private persons gather together outside the government, they will themselves constitute something like a government, so that the prestige of the original government will decline. To this I reply that this is the talk of small-minded men. Persons in both the private and public sectors are equally Japanese citizens. Therefore they only perform their functions from different positions. Actually they both contribute to the country as a whole through their several complementary efforts. They are not enemies, but truly profitable friends. But of course, if these men in the private sector violate the law, we should not have the least hesitation about punishing them.

The fourth objection is that even persons who desire to be privately based have no way to make a decent livelihood outside of government posts. To this I reply that these words are not worthy of scholars and gentlemen. A scholar, one who is concerned with the affairs of the nation, is already a man of no mean accomplishment. There is little danger that he will be forced to live in poverty for lack of talent. There is no reason why public office is an easier road of life than working from a private base. If the former were easier and more profitable than the latter, we should say that there is a disproportion between efforts and rewards. Greed for excessive profit is not the sign of a true gentleman. Persons who cling to public office through no talent of their own, who rely only on good luck, who covet excessive salaries so that they can live in luxury, and who only casually discuss matters of government, will be no friends of mine.

Section
FIVE

As this work was originally presented as a book for the public and as a text for lower schools, I made every effort from the beginning through the third section to use common words, it being my intention to keep the style of writing simple. But in the fourth section I changed my style a bit, using perhaps slightly more difficult vocabulary. And since this fifth section is a written record of a lecture which I delivered on 1 January 1874, at the New Year meeting of Keio colleagues, I fear likewise that its form may also be more difficult.

Both the fourth and fifth sections are essays for scholarly audiences. Present-day scholars are mostly fainthearted, their spirits not firm. But since they can read letters quite well, and they have no trouble even with difficult texts, I have not hesitated to write in a more demanding style in these two sections, and have naturally elevated their meaning as well. Therefore if I have failed in my original resolve of making this work a book for the public, I apologize to my young readers for it. But, for the convenience of lower-school students, I promise from the sixth section on to return again to my original plain style. I pray, therefore, that the relative difficulty of the whole work will not be judged by my readers merely in terms of these two sections.

SPEECH DELIVERED 1 JANUARY 1874

We are gathered here today at the Keio-gijuku this first of January 1874. It is a year of Japanese independence, and this school is an independent school for us Keio colleagues. For Keio-gijuku to reach a new year in this way should be a cause of great joy to us. But should it be lost this cause for joy can turn into sorrow. Therefore while today we celebrate, let us not forget that we may grieve on some future day. Despite changes in government due to war or peace from ancient times down, Japan has never yet lost her independence. For up to today the people of the nation have been satisfied with the custom of national seclusion, her internal political vicissitudes having been unrelated to foreign affairs. Her independence, which was never lost nationally through periods of peaceful rule or civil disorder, was a domestic experience that had not clashed in arms with foreigners. We Japanese have been like children raised within a house who have not yet had contact with the outside world. Our weakness, of course, is self-evident.

But now that trade with foreign nations has suddenly begun, there is no domestic affair that remains unrelated to them. Now all matters must be dealt with in comparison with foreign nations. But Japan's civilization, itself barely attained by our ancestors, is no match with that of the West. We must therefore lament our own inadequacies to follow the ways of the West; at the same time, we must increasingly awaken to the actual dangers to our independence as a nation.

The civilization of a country should not be evaluated in terms of its external forms. Schools, industry, army and navy, are merely external forms of civilization. It is not difficult to create these forms, which can all be purchased with money. But there is additionally a spiritual component, which cannot be seen or heard, bought or sold, lent or borrowed. Yet its influence on the nation is very great. Without it, the schools, industries, and military capabilities lose their meaning. It is indeed the all-important value, i.e. the spirit of civilization. What is, then, this spiritual component, which in turn is the spirit of independence of a people? Recently, the government has repeatedly founded schools, promoted industries, greatly reformed the army and navy systems, and has almost attained modern civilization in outward form. But no one yet considers the problem of strengthening Japanese independence. No one comes forth to lead the rest. Not only that, while they have had rare chances to gain knowledge of other nations, they first of all become afraid of foreign nations before they have accurate information on them. Even if they have something to offer, their fear of others prevents them from bringing it forward. In short, if people lack this spirit of independence, the outward forms of modern civilization are ultimately useless.

The reason for this, in the first place, is that since time immemorial the reins of power in the whole country have been monopolized by the government. From military defense, book learning, to industry and commerce, every insignificant affair of the people has been under governmental jurisdiction. The people have always been the dupes of government. In effect, the country has been the private property of the government, and the people have been the hangers-on of the country. The people, like guests without permanent lodgings, just barely managed a parasitical existence within the country. They looked upon it as a lodging house in which they could neither give full vent to their keenest wishes nor express their full energies. This gradually nurtured the present spiritual climate of Japan. But modern Japan has an even worse problem than this. In all matters of the world, not to go forward is to retreat and, not to retreat is to advance. In principle no one can mark time neither advancing or retreating. In present-day Japan, the external forms of modern civilization seem to have progressed, but the energy of the people, which is the spirit of civilization, is daily retreating.

Let me discuss this point further. In the past regimes of the Ashikaga [1338–1573] and Tokugawa [1600–1868], force alone was used to control the people. The people were obedient to the government because they did not have sufficient power of their own. It is not that they admired the government; they only showed faces of submission out of fear. The present government not only has power, but is resourceful and shrewd as well. There is no area in which it lags behind the times. Not ten years since the Meiji Restoration, the reforms in the educational and military systems, in railroad and telegraph, in construction of concrete buildings and iron bridges, are all attributable to the quickness of governmental decisions. The quality of its accomplishments is in fact astonishing. But they are all exclusively government accomplishments. What regard can the people actually have for them? The people say: Now the government has not only the power but the knowledge as well; both are beyond our power. The government administers the nation from the clouds above, while we citizens can only depend on it from below. It is the function of the government above to be concerned about the country, while we lowly citizens have nothing to do with it.

In sum, the governments of the past used force, but the present regime uses both force and intelligence. In contrast to the former, the latter is rich in techniques of controlling the people. Past governments deprived the people of power; the present regime robs them of their minds. Past governments controlled men externally, the present regime controls their internal life as well. The former was a devil to the people, the latter is now a god. Fear has given place to blind worship. If such abuses of the past are not reformed at this juncture, and the government undertakes something new, the form of civilization may seem to be gradually given shape, but in fact the people will be totally enervated, so that the spirit of civilization will gradually wither away. Today the government has a regular army. The people ought to be in high spirits, regarding it as an army for the protection of the country, and celebrating its splendor. But, on the contrary, they regard it only as another formidable strong arm of the government. The government owns the schools and railroads. The people ought to take pride in these things as symbols of the civilization of the country. But, on the contrary, they attribute it to the benevolence of the government and rely more and more on its largesse. The people are already cowering before the Meiji government. How can they have time to enter into competition with the civilization of the West? Therefore I say that without independent energy, Japan's external forms of civilization will not only be less than useless, but will merely be tools to intimidate men's hearts.

Consequently, the civilization of a nation can be initiated neither from the government above nor from the people below. It must begin from a middle position which expresses the directions of the people as a whole. Success can be expected only after the nation stand on terms of equality with the government. In Western history, not one form of business or industry was the creation of the government. Their foundations were always laid by the projects of scholars in the "middle class." The steam engine was invented by Watt [1736–1819], the railroad was designed by Stephenson [1781–1848]. Adam Smith [1723–90] expounded the principles of economics and completely changed the methods of business. These great scholars belonged to the so-called **middle class**. They were neither government administrators nor the laboring masses. Theirs was exactly that middle position which leads the world by power of intellect. Once some device or invention takes form in someone's mind, a private company is founded to concretize it in practical form. It can then make a lasting contribution to the great happiness of future generations.

At this juncture the duty of the government is to let the creativity of the people take its own course without interference, to understand and protect the direction of public opinion. The people should take the initiative in the affairs of civilization, while the government protects their efforts. The people should own civilization as if it were their private property. They should compete and dispute with one another over its forms. They should take pride in their achievements. The whole nation should respond to each commendable achievement made within the country. Their only fear should be that other nations might beat them to it. In such a situation the matters of civilized progress will all become the instruments of strengthening the spirit of the nation. Everything will be conducive to fostering national independence.

But this state of affairs is the exact contrary of what actually prevails in Japan. At present, the only Japanese in the **middle class** who can advocate national independence and modern civilization are the scholars. But most of these same scholars are unsatisfied with their present positions. They are going into government service instead. They either are not insightful about the trend of the times, or they are more concerned about their own private interests than those of the nation. Or again, they are intoxicated with the spirit of the times which looks to the government to accomplish everything. They engage in trifling businesses involving physical and mental labors. Their conduct is mostly ridiculous. But they are personally self-satisfied; and people do not question them. In the worst extreme, some are saying with pride that there are no talented men working outside the government. People should not be blamed individually, for this is the pernicious spirit of the times. Yet it is a great misfortune for Japanese civilization.

We should bitterly lament the indifference and apathy people are showing to the fact that scholars, who ought to be the leaders of civilization, are spiritually declining day by day. And that the scholars are spiritually declining is even more bitterly deplorable! We colleagues of Keio-gijuku have alone narrowly escaped this calamity. We have cultivated the spirit of independence for these past several years in our own independent institution of learning. And our only desire has been to maintain the independence of the whole nation. But the currents of the times have inundated the land; or it is like a typhoon—it is not easy to stand up against it. Without great personal efforts, a person will unconsciously be swept along with it. But power to resist will not come from book learning alone. Reading is a mere means to learning. Learning issues forth in practice. Power will come only as we actually come to grips with things in concrete life.

Those members of our school who have realized this in practice should apply their knowledge, no matter what the personal cost, to the actual advance of Japanese civilization. Fields to work in are too numerous to mention. Business, law, industry, agriculture, the writing and translation of books, publication of newspapers—almost every affair of civilization—must be made our own. We must take the lead of the people, and act in concert with the government, so that the proper balance of powers of the public and the private will increase the potential of the whole nation. In this way, we shall be able to firm up the faltering condition of Japan's independence, so that we can hold our ground unflinchingly in the event of war with a foreign nation. If years from hence we were to look back with pity on our present lack of independence rather than taking pride in it, would this not be a most happy turn of events? Let scholars therefore set their goals with confidence.

Section
SIX

THE IMPORTANCE OF NATIONAL LAWS

The government represents the people. It conducts its affairs in accordance with the wishes of the people. Its duty is to arrest those who commit crimes, and to protect those who are innocent. This is what the people desire. Therefore if this purpose can be achieved, the government will be serving the country well. For, in the first place, criminals are wicked, and the innocent are good. There is therefore no reason to object if a good person defends himself against the wicked intentions of another—for example, if that wicked person had attempted to harm the good person, to kill the good person's own loved ones, or to rob his household, it will not be unreasonable if the good person apprehends the wicked person, and perhaps kills him or whips him. But it would be quite impossible to defend oneself against a whole lot of wicked people at once; or again, even if he could, it would involve an extravagantly great expense. Therefore a government is founded to represent the people, and to perform the service of protecting the people. In compensation for this service, the people have promised to pay all the expenses of the government, not to speak of the wages of the officials.

Furthermore, since the government has become the representative of the people and has acquired the right to act in their behalf, its measures are the people's measures, and accordingly the people must obey the law. This is a contract between the people and the government. Hence obedience to the nation's government by the people means, not obedience to laws enacted by the government, but obedience to laws enacted by themselves. Violation of the nation's laws means, not violation of the government's laws, but violation of their own laws. Punishment for violation of the law means punishment by the laws which they themselves have set up. It is as if each citizen performed the duties of two persons. The first duty is to found a government to represent the people by arresting the wicked and protecting the innocent. The second is strictly to obey the covenant they have made with the government, and thus to receive its protection in accordance with the law.

As I have just said, since the people have contracted to entrust the authority of the law to the government, they may on no account disobey the law, thereby violating the terms of that contract. It is the right of the government to arrest and execute a murderer. It is the right of the government to arrest and put a robber in prison, as well as to settle lawsuits, to prevent violence and disputes. The people must not interfere with these prerogatives to any degree. If, in ignorance of this principle, a person should take it upon himself privately to execute a murderer or to arrest and lash a robber, it would be rendering a private decision on the other person's crime as well as violating the law of the land. This is called a private punishment, the crime of which is unpardonable. In this case of private vendetta, the laws of civilized countries are exceedingly severe. They exercise authority without being brutal. In Japan, the authority of the government seems to be prestigious, but some people only fear its superior position, while still not understanding the intrinsic value of the laws in themselves. So let me further explain why private punishment is wrong, and why national laws are intrinsically valuable.

Let us suppose that a burglar enters your house and tries to rob your money by threatening your family. At such a time, the duty of the master of the house is to make a formal complaint to the government and await its disposal of the criminal. But since the present matter is too urgent, there is no time to appeal to the courts. In the meanwhile the burglar has proceeded to enter the storehouse and is about to abscond with your money. If the master of the house tries to stop him, he may endanger his life. Therefore the family must prevent this from happening by taking private steps. They have the temporary right to apprehend the thief, and then appeal to the government. They may have to use a knife or stick which wounds the thief or breaks his leg. In an extreme emergency, they may have to shoot him. But this is the case of the master of the house taking temporary measures to defend himself and his household. It is not an accusation against the thief's wrongdoing, and it is not a direct punishment of his crime. The government alone can punish the criminal; it is not a duty entrusted to the private individual. Therefore, even if one has privately apprehended a robber, he may not kill or lash him. He may not even lay a finger on him. He must report it to the government and abide by its decision. If he kills the thief out of anger, or lashes him, his own crime will be no less than killing or lashing an innocent person.

According to one country's laws, a person who steals ten yen will receive a punishment of one hundred thrashings; kicking another's face will likewise draw a punishment of one hundred thrashings. Now consider the case in which a thief breaks into another's house and steals ten yen. As he is about to run away, he is captured and tied up by the master of the house. After that, the master of the house kicks the robber's face. According to the laws of that country, the robber should receive one hundred thrashings for stealing ten yen, and the master of the house should also receive one hundred thrashings for his own crime of opting privately to kick him in the face out of anger. Such is the severity of the law of that nation. People must take heed of it.

From the above principle it can be understood that private vengeance is evil.† The murderer of one's own parent is officially a criminal of the state. The government alone has the official duty to arrest and condemn this criminal. No civilian should be involved. In no instance can even the son of the murdered parent take it upon himself to kill this criminal in place of the government. This would be not only an imprudent conduct on his part but it would also be to mistake his duty as a citizen of the nation, and to violate his contract made with the government. If the government disposes of the case with undue favoritism to the accused, the son should complain of this injustice to the government. Whatever reasons one may have, one is not entitled on any account to initiate the process of punishment. Even if the murderer of one's parent is lingering before his own eyes, he has no right to retaliate privately.

---

† [In 1873, the Meiji government enforced the law banning any crimes of revenge.]

In the Tokugawa Period, the retainers of Lord Asano killed Kira Kōzuke-no-suke to avenge the death of their master.[†] People praised them as loyal samurai of Akō. But was this not a great error? The Tokugawa shogunate constituted the government at that time. Both Asano Takumi-no-kami and Kira Kōzuke-no-suke, and the retainers of the Asano house as well, were all Japanese citizens. They had promised the government to obey its laws, and thus to receive the government's protection under the law. However, by some mistake Kira insulted Asano. But the latter did not lodge a complaint with the government; in anger, he attempted to kill Kira directly. This led to a dispute, which ended with the Tokugawa government putting Asano on trial and ordering him to commit *seppuku*. It did not punish Kira. This was a very unjust aspect of the trial. But if the retainers of Lord Asano thought this trial unjust, why did they not complain about it to the goverment?

Now, if each of the forty-seven retainers had made arrangement to lodge a complaint with the authorities according to the law, they might have won their case in the end. The lawsuit might not have been accepted at first, because the government was despotic all along. The first complainant might even have been arrested and killed. But then a second retainer of the Asano house might have stepped fearlessly forward to lodge a second complaint. If all the forty-seven retainers had exposed their lives in their effort to make a just appeal, the government, no matter how bad it was, would eventually have submitted to reason. To make the decision of the trial fairer, it would then have punished Kira as well. By such a procedure the retainers of Asano would have shown how truly loyal they were. But they did not know this principle. In their status as only people of the country, they disregarded the value of the laws of the country to murder Kira out of enmity against a political enemy. By privately deciding another's crime they therefore violated their duties as citizens and trespassed on the right of the government. Fortunately, they were then condemned to death by the Tokugawa

---

† [Fukuzawa is referring to the Akō Vendetta (1702). Asano Naganori (1667–1701), daimyo of Akō, was sentenced to perform *seppuku* (*hara-kiri*) for wounding an official of the bakufu named Kira Yoshihisa (Kira Kō-zuke-no-suke, 1641–1702) in the court. The Asano Clan was consequently abolished, and the forty-seven *rōnin* (masterless samurai) of Asano plotted revenge on Kira and killed him. They were all sentenced to perform *seppuku*.]

authorities, so that the matter was settled. If their crime had been condoned, the retainers of the Kira family would surely have taken their own revenge on the retainers of Akō. One vendetta would have followed another until finally all the kinsmen and friends of both sides would have been wiped out. The result would have been a world of anarchy. Such, then, is the harm of private punishment to the nation; it has no place in the proper conduct of things.

In the past, when Japanese peasants or townsfolk were rude to a samurai, he had the legal right to cut them down with his sword. This right entailed public approbation of private punishment. It was abominable. The laws of the nation must be directly enforced by the government alone. The more numerous the places where laws are enacted, the weaker their power. During the feudal period, when each of the three hundred daimyo held the power of life and death over their people, the power of the Tokugawa government was proportionately weaker too.

Assassination is the worst form of private punishment and is most harmful to the government. Looking at the records from ancient times, we find that some were undertaken out of personal enmity, others to rob money. One who plots such an assassination is from the start an intended criminal. Another kind of assassination is done, not for private motives, but against a **political enemy**. People's political opinions may vary, but some seem to think that they can take their own opinion as the criterion for deciding another's crime. They therefore kill others at will, infringing upon the prerogative of the government. Not only are they not ashamed of their act, they even boast of having inflicted "Heaven's punishment." They are even called patriotic by some.

But what, first of all, is this "Heaven's punishment"? Does it mean to inflict the death penalty in place of Heaven? If that were so, one should first examine his own situation. Living in this land from the beginning, what kind of promise has he made with the government? It was to obey the national laws without fail, and thus to receive the protection of the government. If he has some complaint about certain laws, or thinks that some persons are subversive to the nation, he should quietly lodge a formal complaint with the government. But to bypass the government to take action by oneself in the name of Heaven would be the wrongest kind of solution. No matter how sincere, such persons are ignorant of the principles of things. They worry about the country without truly knowing why. In point of fact, no one has ever accomplished anything good by assassination, or increased the well-being of society thereby.

People who do not understand the intrinsic value of laws live only in fear of the government officials. They do not feel ashamed of having committed a real crime as long as it does not become publicly known. Such lawbreakers who cleverly dodge the law will, on the contrary, sometimes be praised for their cleverness. In the conversations of people we hear such talk as: "While there is a firm law of the land, and an official law of the government, if certain things can be secretly 'arranged' in such and such a way, it will not publicly interfere with the law, and so it can remain an official secret." Thus they talk smilingly, and no one suspects anything. Some go so far as to confer with minor officials to arrange a secret "deal." Both parties seem to benefit from the deal, and there seems to be no crime involved. The immutable laws of the land are in fact too complicated and hard to put into practice, so that such secret deals are liable to be made. But from the standpoint of the nation, this kind of thing is a most dangerous abuse.

If people get the habit of disregarding the law in this way, this spirit of insincerity will become universal. Laws which would be beneficial, if obeyed, will be violated, and crime will be the order of the day. Take for example the government law that prohibits urinating on the roads. Some people do not understand the value of this prohibition. They are only afraid of being caught by the police. If a person is unexpectedly caught by a policeman when furtively breaking this law in the evening, he bows before the law; but within his heart he does not consider that he is being punished for a violation of the law. He only thinks that it was his unlucky day for being nabbed in the act. This is indeed very deplorable. Therefore, when the government makes laws, they must be made simple; and once enacted, they must be strictly enforced to achieve their purpose. If such laws are inconvenient, the people should freely discuss and complain about them to the authorities. Once they have accepted the laws, they must respectfully obey them.

A case came up recently here at Keio-gijuku. Mr. Ōta Sukeyoshi, a peer, had used his own private funds two years ago to hire an American to teach at the Keio. At the expiration of that appointment, he wanted to hire another American. An agreement was informally settled between Mr. Ōta and the interested party. Mr. Ōta then sent a written application to the Tokyo prefecture government office to hire this American as a teacher of the humanities. But a law on the books of the Ministry of Education required that even a private institution could not hire a private instructor who did not have in his possession a diploma showing the completion of his course work in his native land. The American did not have his diploma with him in Japan. Mr. Ōta received official notice that it was permissible to hire him as a language teacher, but not as an instructor in the humanities. Thereupon, I wrote a letter of application to the prefectural office. I said that I was requesting acceptance of Mr. Ōta's application after rendering a favorable judgment on the American's scholastic competence, despite the fact that he does not have his diploma with him to present. I pointed out that the prefectural office would have simply passed on the application if it had been for language teaching. But since our students had from the first desired to study the humanities, we had not taken the trouble to deceive the authorities by using the pretext that he was to be a language teacher. My own application was returned to me with the explanation that the regulation of the Ministry of Education could not be changed. As a result the school had to terminate its negotiations with the prospective teacher. At the end of last December the American returned to the United States. Mr. Ōta's original good intention came to nought, and several hundred students lost a good opportunity to learn. This was indeed not only a great misfortune for a private institution, but also a great drawback to studies in general for the nation. It was a stupid and irksome matter, but the law is important and primary. I intend to make another application in a few days.

Recently Mr. Ōta and the staff of Keio-gijuku informally convened to discuss this case. Since the Ministry of Education's regulation was written in stone, it was suggested more than once that the application should be changed to "language instructor" to have it accepted. But in the end we did not hire the teacher. We decided that the best course of action was to respect and obey the law as befits our position, even if it was a setback for the school. For it is dishonorable for scholars and gentlemen to deceive the government. Of course, this decision may seem to be a mere trifling episode in the life of a single private institution. But I think that the principle at stake is relevant to public morals, and I am taking this opportunity to underline it here.

Section
SEVEN

THE DUTIES OF THE CITIZENS OF THE NATION

In section six I discussed the importance of national laws, saying that each citizen plays two roles in regard to them. I continue that discussion here, elaborating in even greater detail the function and duty of citizens.

Each citizen has a double role. The first is to be subordinate to the government with the mentality of a guest. The second is to join together with the other citizens of the nation to form a company, as it were, that is called the nation, to enact and implement the laws of the nation. This involves the mentality of being a master. For example, if a hundred merchants form some commercial company, establish the rules of the company and implement them, then the hundred merchants are the masters of that company. But once the national laws have been established, the said merchants become guests of that company as well, and must obey those laws. The nation is like a company, and its citizens like the colleagues of the company. Each individual plays the roles of both master and guest.

I To take up first their status as guests: the citizens of a nation must honor the laws of the land, and not forget the principle of the equality of men. If I do not want my rights violated by others, then I must in turn not infringe upon the rights of others. Since others enjoy the same things as I do, I must not take my pleasure by robbing from those of others. I must not steal to enrich myself. I must not kill or slander another. I must correctly uphold the law, and live according to the great principle of the equality of men. Again, there is no reason recklessly to violate laws enacted by the government, even if they are stupid or inconvenient to me. The government has the authority to declare war and conclude treaties with foreign nations. As this authority was originally conferred to the government from the nation under a contract, a person not connected with the administration of the government should not criticize its conduct. If this principle is forgotten, and people think that the measures of the government do not suit their own private liking, or if they criticize it as they wish, thus violating their agreement with the government, or if they raise up arms in revolt against the government, then the government of a country will not last a single day.

Let me go back to my analogy of the company of the hundred merchants. On the basis of common agreement, they elect ten men within the company to be its managers. If the directives of those managers do not please the private opinions of the remaining ninety, so that each criticizes the rules of the company, and goes out to purchase sweet rice cake wholesale while the managers want to sell sake, many different decisions will be taken at once. If they begin to negotiate for the sweet rice cake on their own private initiative, thus violating the laws of the company and conflicting with the others, the business of the company will also not last a single day. As the company finally goes bankrupt, its loss will be suffered equally by each of the one hundred members. Avowedly this is a most stupid thing to do. In like manner, even if the laws of a country are unjust and inconvenient, there is no reason to take that as an excuse to break them. If there are actually points which are unjust and inconvenient, people should peacefully state their case to the government, who are the managers of the country, in order to have these laws amended. If the government does not accede to their private view, the people should do what they can, and at the same time be patient, waiting for the proper time to come.

II To take up secondly their status as masters, the citizens of a nation are at the same time the government itself. Since not every person can directly administer the affairs of state, that is entrusted to the government, which contracts to serve as the representative of the people. Accordingly, the people are the real masters and bosses; the government is their representative and manager. In our example, the ten men elected by the commercial company of a hundred merchants are the government, the remaining ninety are the people. The ninety do not directly run the affairs of the company which they have delegated to their representatives. But if they consider their own status, they cannot help but call themselves the actual bosses of the company. Again, the ten managers who execute the present affairs of the company have been entrusted to execute business according to the will of the whole company; therefore, they are not making private decisions but official ones of the company. Similarly, the affairs of government are not private affairs of government officials, but are public affairs of the nation as a whole executed by the representatives of the people.

The government receives the mandate of the people. According to its role in the contract, it must seek to promote the rights of all, without distinction between noble and base and high and low, and must not exhibit even one degree of injustice and selfishness in its correct application of the law and punishment of crime. If bandits should illegally break into a person's house, but the government is incapable of controlling them, then it can be said to be in collusion with the bandits. If the government cannot fulfill the principles of the national law, and causes the people to suffer financial losses, it must make reparations, irrespective of amount and age. Thus, for example, if a government official, through his own negligence, was responsible for a loss incurred by a citizen or a foreigner, he should have to pay a reparation of, say, thirty thousand yen. Since in principle the government does not have its own money, the ones who ultimately pay the bill are, of course, the people. If this thirty thousand yen is proportioned among the Japanese population of thirty million, it comes to ten *mon* per person. If the negligence of the official costs ten times as much, each citizen ends up paying one hundred *mon*. That would amount to five hundred *mon* in a family of five. If the poor farmers in the rural districts had five hundred *mon* to spend, they could call their wives and children together to celebrate an appropriate feast, and spend the whole night in merriment. Would it not be a miserable thing if through the negligence of one public official the innocent people throughout Japan would be forced to be deprived of their greatest of pleasures? It is unreasonable that the citizens themselves have to foot the bill for such stupidity, but what can be done about it? They themselves are the masters and bosses. They originally contracted to entrust the handling of affairs to the government. Since both losses and gains are to be shared by the masters, they cannot be critical of the carelessness of the officials only when they lose money. Therefore the people must always be careful. If they are anxious in heart at the dealings of the government, they should peacefully and frankly state their cases.

Since the people are already the masters of the country, it is their essential obligation to pay for the expenses taken to protect the country. They should hardly grumble over this. To protect the country, salaries must be paid to officials, army and navy appropriations made, and there will be expenses for the law courts and local officials as well. The total sum of this amount seems very great, but it is not so bad if apportioned among the total population. Annual tax revenue in Japan comes to only one or two yen per person. To pay this small amount in return for the protection of the government, so as not to have to fear night burglars or bandits when travelling alone, and to be able to pass one's whole life in peace and security, is indeed a great bargain.

There are relatively profitable businesses everywhere, but there would seem to be nothing as economical as buying the protection of the government through paying taxes. Nowadays there are men spending money on building houses, and striving to acquire the finest clothes and foods. Even worse, there are people ruining their fortunes on amusements and pleasures. The money these people spend is incomparably more than the amount of taxes they pay. If it is spent illicitly, they should hesitate to spend even a single sen. But since tax revenue is money spent not only rightfully, but to purchase the most economical of things, they should pay their taxes gladly.

It is an ideal situation when both the people and the government fulfill their respective roles and come to a mutual understanding in the above way. But when this is not the actual situation, those who are the government may transcend their limits to execute a tyrannical rule. In that instance, the people have only three courses of action. First, they may surrender their integrity and submit to the government. Secondly, they may resist the government by force of arms. Thirdly, they may go as far as sacrificing their lives to uphold the principle of justice.

The first of these courses of action would be extremely immoral. It is the duty of the people to obey the just Way of Heaven. But when they surrender their integrity to follow the evil ways contrived by the government, they are violating their duties as men. Moreover, when they surrender their integrity to obey such laws, they create corrupt practices in the country as a whole by leaving a legacy of evil precedents to their children. Since ancient times, there have been tyrannical governments over stupid people in Japan as well. If the government moved to extend its empty prestige, the people shook with fear. They knew that the government's dealings were actually unjust, but they were afraid that if they clearly voiced an opinion about it, the government would become incensed, or they would be made secretly to suffer by the officials in the future. Thus they did not say what should have been said. They cringed as if the officials would rub their noses in dog duty. The people were afraid of such a ludicrous reprisal. Their mentality was to bend before the government, no matter how unjust. Their spirit permeated the whole society which has finally fallen into the wretched condition of today. When they surrendered their integrity, they bequeathed calamity to their descendants.

The second recourse is to resist the government by force of arms. Of course, this requires many men, and therefore political cliques must inevitably be formed. This gives rise to civil war. And therefore such a course of action cannot be called the best policy. For the time being the question of right and wrong must be set aside, and, once war has been declared, we need only consider which side has more power. If we survey the history of rebellions in both past and modern times, the power of the people has always been weaker than that of the government. If they do rise up in rebellion, they should of course overthrow the past framework of the government. But no matter how corrupt the old regime was, if the new one is also such, there would be no justification for it to hold the reins of power for even a few years. Even if they overthrow it out of temporary impulse, it would only be to substitute one form of stupidity and tyranny with another. Moreover, civil wars are caused by the inhumane treatment inflicted upon the people in the past.

But there is nothing more inhumane than civil war. The bonds between friends are torn asunder; worse, parents and children become each other's killers, brothers become each other's enemies; homes are burnt down and people slaughtered—thus, evil deeds run rampant. In such frightful circumstances people's hearts become inured to cruelty. As they perform actions which may be called almost beast-like, will they aspire to administer affairs better than the old government, to lighten the burden of the law, so that they can lead the people of the whole country to walk the path of benevolence and human sentiment? I say that such thoughts are wrong.

The third course of action is to be prepared to sacrifice one's life to uphold just principles. This entails trusting confidently in the principle of Heaven. It entails that no matter how bitter the law under which individuals are made to suffer by a tyrannical government, they endure that suffering without letting their spirits break. Neither taking up arms nor using even the slightest degree of violence, they only bring pressure to bear upon the government by advocating just principles. And this third way must be said to be the best policy. If rational pressure is brought to bear upon the government, the existing good administration and laws will not at all be harmed. Their just arguments may perhaps not be adopted, but since it is clear that they stand to reason, the innate sentiment of men will be swayed by them. What is not accomplished this year will be accomplished in the following year. Moreover, there is danger that resistance against the government through force of arms will destroy a hundred things in pursuit of one goal, whereas rational persuasion will sweep out only those evils that should be eliminated, without creating additional troubles. Since their objective is to put an end to governmental injustice, criticism can be stopped as the government returns to just ways. Further, armed resistance will bring angry counter-resistance. Instead of reconsidering its own evils, the government will brandish its tyrannical power all the more, even resorting to further force. But as even a tyrannical government and its officials are citizens of the same country, the sight of their fellow countrymen quietly advocating truth by sacrificing their own lives to uphold the principles of justice will ultimately win their hearts. Once this happens, they will repent of their own wrongdoings, naturally throw off their arrogance, and reform their ways.

Such persons who are concerned about their country and undergo sufferings or even sacrifice their lives because of it, are called **martyrs** in the West. Although a martyr gives only his own life, his accomplishment is superior to a civil war which kills innumerable others and costs an incalculable sum of money. Since ancient times, many Japanese have died on the battlefield or committed *seppuku*. They have all been highly praised as loyal retainers. But the reason for their heroic deaths was in most cases related to a war between two lords who were vying for political supremacy, or to perform some vendetta for their lord. To give one's life so nobly may seem in outward appearance to be admirable, but in actual fact it was of no benefit to society. The idea that the mere sacrifice of one's life is everything, whether it is for the sake of one's lord or out of apology to him, is common in illiterate and uncivilized societies. But in the light of modern civilization, such people must be said not to have known the true reason for sacrificing their lives.

In essence, civilization means to advance the levels of knowledge and virtue of the people, so that each and every person can be the master of his own affairs in his dealings with society. It means that, without harm to either side, every person enjoys his own rights and thereby contributes to the security and prosperity of all.

In this light, were civil wars or vendettas actually in accord with the purpose of civilization? Dying in battle or in a vendetta may seem to have been rational if there was the sure prospect that the society would be enabled to become more civilized by creating business and industry and contributing to the general security and prosperity—that is, only through the agency of winning a civil war and destroying the enemy, or accomplishing the vendetta and saving the lord's honor. But in actual fact these were never the goals. Probably even the famous loyal retainers did not entertain such intentions. They must have acted only out of bounden obligation and apology to their lords.

Indeed, if we call "loyal retainers" such people who sacrifice their lives out of apology to their masters, there are many such examples in society even today. A certain servant, while on an errand for his master, loses one *ryō* of gold. At his wit's end, he decides that he cannot apologize, and so he ties his loincloth to the branch of a tree and hangs himself. If we truly consider this loyal servant's frame of mind when he resolved to kill himself, we must pity him. He went out on an errand, but took his own life before returning. He thus becomes an eternal hero whose story makes us moisten our sleeves with tears. To kill oneself to fulfill the master-servant relationship after having lost one *ryō* of gold received in trust is no less noble than the stories of the loyal retainers of the past and present. However, while his loyalty should shine bright like the sun and the moon, and his meritorious deed should be eternal with the heaven and the earth, people are all coldhearted and belittle this servant. They make no memorial stone to commemorate his deed, and build no shrine to worship him. Why is this? People will say, "Because the servant's death was merely for the one *ryō* of gold. The reason was too trivial."

But we cannot discuss the relative gravity of a deed merely in terms of the amount of money or number of persons involved. Our criterion should be whether it was beneficial to the advance of civilization. Though the loyal samurai died in battle while killing ten thousand of the enemy and poor Gonsuke hanged himself for losing one *ryō* of gold, they were truly the same in regard to the fact that neither of them benefited civilization through their deaths. Since neither can be more highly evaluated, we may say that neither knew the true reasons for giving their lives. Neither can either be called a **martyr**. From what I know, there was only one person from ancient times who advocated human rights, who brought pressure to bear upon the government by championing the cause of justice, and who remained steadfast and kept his integrity to the end, when he sacrificed his life. This was Sakura Sōgorō,[†] whose biography is found only in popular fiction handed down by the people, but whose true story has still not been told by the historians. Some future day, if his history becomes clear, I shall record it and reveal his merits and virtues, to offer them as a model to men.

---

† Sakura Sōgorō (1605?–53?) was a public-spirited headman of a village in the domain of Sakura in the province of Shimousa.

Section
EIGHT

RESPECT FOR THE INDEPENDENCE OF OTHERS

In the work entitled *Moral Science* by the American named Francis Wayland [1796–1865], there is a discussion of the freedom of the human mind and body. The general point of this book is that each individual constitutes an independent person who is the master of his own affairs, uses his own mind and does his own necessary business. Therefore:

a) Every person has a physical body through which he comes in contact with external things which he uses to meet his own needs. For example, he can plant seeds to grow rice, or make clothes from cotton.

b) Every person has an intellect through which he can discover the principles of things to guide him in doing things. For example, he can devise methods of fertilization for rice cultivation, or design a loom to weave cotton thread. These are functions of intelligence and discernment.

c) Every person has desires, through which he activates the functions of mind and body. By satisfying these desires he can achieve happiness. For example, every human being loves fine clothes and delicious foods. Still, these things are not natural products of the earth. Men must work to make them. Therefore, human action arises from the spur of human desires, which are the necessary catalysts for action. These actions, in turn, are the indispensable conditions for attaining happiness. It may be said that such persons as Zen priests have neither actions nor happiness.

d) Every person has a conscience, which controls his desires, turns his tendencies in the right direction, and decides where to curb them. For example, human desires are limitless. It is difficult indeed to set limits on the pursuit of fine clothes and delicious foods. But if one were to neglect his necessary business in an exclusive pursuit of his heart's desires, he would inevitably try to profit at the expense of others. This cannot be called a truly human course of action. At such a time it is the honest conscience that distinguishes between desires and the truth, and prompts man to live within the truth.

e) Every man has a will, through which he can decide to act. For example, things cannot be accomplished by chance. Good and evil are the results of the striving of the human will.

The above five characteristics are indispensable for being a true man. A person must freely employ them to attain personal independence. When I say independence, it may seem that I am talking about some kind of eccentric and strange people who live in isolation from society. But this is hardly so. To live in the world as a human being one must have friends. But these friends in turn seek relationships with me, just as I seek their company. Therefore our relations are mutual. But when a person employs the above five qualities of mankind, the most important is to obey the laws established by Heaven, without overstepping his limit and capacity. By limit and capacity I mean that neither I nor another should use these qualities to infringe upon the activities of each other. Thus one will neither be blamed by other people nor punished by Heaven if he can pass his life without overstepping his limits as a human being. This is what the rights of man are about.

The above argument sets down the principles whereby a man can conduct himself in freedom, as long as he does not infringe upon the rights of others. He can go or stay as he pleases, work or play, engage in some business, study hard day and night or, if that does not agree with him, loaf around the whole day long. Provided these actions do not affect others, there is no reason for men to censure them from the sidelines.

Now, let us suppose that there are some persons who oppose the above ideas. Their opinion may be that one should act in obedience to the will of others, irrespective of the right or wrong of things, and that it is not good to express one's own mind. How reasonable is this kind of argument? If it were reasonable, it should be universally valid for all men in the world. Let me illustrate. Since the emperor has greater dignity than the shogun, he should have been able to tell the shogun what to do, how to act, when to eat and sleep, etc., in a quite arbitrary manner as he so wished him to do. The shogun in turn should have coerced the daimyos below him; he should have freely dealt with them according to his own pleasure. The daimyos should have done the same to their house elders, these house elders to their attendants, these attendants to their low-ranking samurai, these low-ranking samurai to the *ashigaru*, and the *ashigaru* to the peasants, all the way down the line. But this argument is somewhat nonplussed when it comes to the peasants, for there are none below them. Yet it was supposed to be universally valid from the beginning, like the principle of the revolving rosary of *One Million Recitations of the Nenbutsu* that must always revolve full circle. The peasants are as much human beings as the emperor. Therefore what if the peasants do not hesitate to treat the emperor at will according to their own pleasure? For example, suppose they tell the emperor to stop when he wants to visit some place; they tell him to go back when he wants to go to his villa. Or suppose that the emperor's daily life was controlled by the arbitrary directives of the peasants, who deprive him of his fine clothes and substitute boiled barley for his delicious foods. In that eventuality, the Japanese would be a people who had the right to control others, but not to control themselves. It would be as if a person's body and mind were two completely different entitites and the body were a place to lodge another's soul; perhaps a strong drinker's soul in a non-drinker's body, or an old man's soul in a child's, or a robber's soul in Confucius's body, or a hunter's soul in Śākyamuni's. It would be as if a non-drinker had a good time drinking sake, while a strong drinker were satisfied in drinking warm sugared water; or an old man enjoyed climbing a tree, while a child walked with a stick and meddled in other people's business; or Confucius led his pupils to commit robbery and Śākyamuni carried a gun and went out hunting. The results would be incongruous indeed! They would be strange, and unimaginable.

Shall we call this heavenly principle and human nature? Or civilization and enlightenment? Even a child of three could answer. The duties of both high and low expounded by the scholars of Chinese and Japanese Learning from time immemorial have served to install someone else's soul into one's own body. They have been teaching this kind of thing, even admonishing people with tears, and they have gradually borne fruit in these degenerate days. As it has become customary for the strong to control the weak, the scholars too are showing faces of pride. The divinities of the Age of the Gods and the sages of the Zhou must be resting happily in their graves. Let me take up one or two of their so-called meritorious teachings below.

I shall not repeat here my position in regard to the argument that a strong government should dominate over weak subjects. Let me here take up the question of the relations between men and women. In the first place, they are both born as human beings. Because both man and woman have roles indispensable for life, without them the world cannot endure even a day. Their capabilities are about the same, but men are generally stronger than women. If a strong man fights a woman he will always win. In society, a person who steals by force or who puts another to shame is called a criminal, and is punished. Why, then, is it that a man may openly put others to shame within the family without even being reproached for it?

In a book called "Onna daigaku" (The Great Learning for Women) there is enunciated a principle of "triple obedience" for women: a) to obey her parents when young, b) to obey her husband when married, and c) to obey her children when old. It may be natural for a girl to obey her parents when she is young, but in what way is she to obey her husband after marriage? I am curious about that! The book says that even if the husband is a drunkard or is addicted to sensual pleasures, or abuses and scolds her, and thus goes to the extreme of dissipation and lechery, the wife must still be obedient. She must respect her dissolute husband like Heaven, and only protest to him with kind words and soft countenance. This is as far as the book goes. It says not a word about the outcome after this. It would therefore seem that its teaching is that as long as one has become a husband, his wife must obey him, even if he is dissolute or an adulterer, and no matter what her disgrace. She can only remonstrate with him with a gentle countenance, contrary to her real mind. The dissolute husband may follow her remonstrances or not. She is forced to consider her dissolute husband's mind as her fate. A Buddhist scripture says that "Women are full of sins." Indeed, from this point of view, women are from birth no other than criminals who have committed great crimes. At the same time, the book severely criticizes women and gives seven reasons for divorcing a wife. It clearly states its reasons, and says that if she is lustful, it is grounds for divorce. This is very convenient for men. But it is entirely one-sided. In the last analysis, it is a teaching that sets up moral obligations between high and low, i.e. between men and women, on the basis of might makes right. For men are stronger than women.

The above-cited passages refer to adulterers and wanton women, but the book also has a discussion of concubines. By nature's decree, the number of male and female births seem to be about equal. According to some statistics in the West, more males are born than females, the proportion being twenty two males to every twenty females. Accordingly, it is clearly against the law of nature when one husband has two or three wives. We should not hesitate to call such men beasts. Those who have a common father and mother are called brothers and sisters, and the place where parents and children live is called a home. But here there are brothers who have a common father but different mothers. There is only one father but a group of mothers. Can we call this a truly human home? It is not worthy of that name. Even if the house is many-storied and lofty, and the rooms are all beautiful, it is to me more like a shed for animals than a home for human beings. From ancient times we have never heard of a harmonious home with a plurality of wives. Even if a man keeps a secret mistress, she is a human being just the same. A person who uses a human being like a beast just for the pleasures of the moment, who disturbs the customs of the family and harms the education of his children and grandchildren, who spreads evils all over the country and leaves poison to future generations, must indeed be called a criminal.

Someone may counter that if a man supports a number of mistresses, there will be no violation of human nature if he treats them properly. This is the opinion of Confucius himself. If what he says were true, a woman should be allowed to support a number of husbands. She should be able to call them male concubines, and give them lower-ranking positions in the household. What then? If a woman could manage her household under such conditions without violating the great principle of social relations, I will stop my chattering arguments once and for all.

Men throughout the whole land should look into their own hearts. But someone may say that "It is to acquire an heir that one supports a mistress." According to Mencius, there are three kinds of impiety to one's parents, and not to have an heir is the most impious. To this I reply that any one who advocates ideas contrary to the natural law, even if he be Mencius or Confucius, should unhesitatingly be called a criminal. What a shame to marry a woman, and to call her most impious if she does not bear a child! Even if it is only a pretext, is it not terrible? What person with a human heart could believe this wild talk of Mencius?

In the first place, lack of filial piety means to do something that is against reason which displeases one's parents. Of course, the old are happy to have grandchildren, but this is no reason to call a person unfilial if a grandchild's birth is late. To the parents of the whole country I ask: when your son marries a good wife, do you get angry at her because she does not bear a child, and do you beat your son and wish to disown him? In this wide world there would be no queerer kind of parents. But these are all empty theories from the first, which are not worth answering. People can find the answers to these questions in their own hearts.

It is natural for a human being to be dutiful to his parents. Even strangers treat old persons with politeness. Much more should a son love his parents. He should be filial to his parents, not for the sake of profit or name, but out of natural sincerity, simply because they are his parents. There are many stories in Japan and China from ancient times that encourage filial piety, beginning with the story of the *Twenty-four Paragons of Filial Piety*. But when we look at these stories, eight or nine out of ten encourage things which are too difficult to do, or things which are too foolish and ridiculous. Even worse, they sometimes praise things which are irrational as acts of filial piety. To lie on the ice in midwinter with no clothing on, and wait for the ice to melt—as one story has it—is impossible for a human being. Or instead of pouring sake over one's body on a summer evening to attract the mosquitoes away from one's parents—as another story has it—would it not be wiser to buy a paper mosquito net for the price of the sake? Or the man who buried his innocent child alive because he had no way to support his parents must have had the heart of a devil or viper. Such persons violate natural law and human nature.

We just saw that Mencius says there are three kinds of unfiliality, and that the most filial impiety is not to have an heir. Now we read that a man, out of filial piety to his parents, tries to bury his child alive. Which is the real instance of filial piety? Or are they both not false theories and self-contradictory? In the last analysis, such theories which endeavor to clarify the duties between parents and children, and high and low, and to establish rank relationships end up forcibly devaluing the child. They give such reasons as that the child has been a source of pain to the mother during pregnancy and childbirth, or that it cannot be separated from its parents for three years after birth. They therefore say that it owes a great debt of gratitude. But not only human beings but even the birds and the beasts all bear young and support them. The only difference is that human parents must educate their children and teach them the ways of social life in addition to providing daily necessities.

Parents give birth to children easily enough, but they do not know the principles of educating them. The father indulges in dissipation, gives a bad example to his children, and drags the family down into poverty and disgrace. He becomes stubborn as his spirit gradually declines and the family fortune shrinks away to nought. He then forces his son to be dutiful. What kind of a shameless scene is this? He is now craving after his son's money. The mother-in-law torments the heart of her daughter-in-law. Both elder parents control their son and his wife according to their own desires. The unreasonable parents are always right, the protests of the son are always wrong. The daughter-in-law has no freedom the whole day through, as if she were in a hungry devil's hell. Whenever she does anything contrary to her husband's parents' wishes, she is called an impious daughter. People may think this is unjust, but since it does not involve them personally, they side with the unreasonable parents. Or some persons advise the son to deceive his parents, regardless of right and wrong. Can we really call this the correct principles of family living? I once said that the mother-in-law should look back upon her younger days when she was a daughter-in-law and make it a good lesson. She ought to recall her own younger days, instead of tormenting her daughter-in-law.

I have given above two examples of the evil which results from the doctrine of subordination between high and low and noble and base—first, in regard to the husband-and-wife relationship, and secondly, between parents and children. These evils are widespread in society. They seep into every aspect of human social relations. I shall give further examples of these abuses in the next section.

Section
NINE

A LETTER TO OLD FRIENDS IN NAKATSU STATING TWO WAYS OF LEARNING

Carefully considering the mental and physical functions of mankind, I find that I can make the following division: the functions of individual persons and those of social beings.

Let us call the former function the pursuit of happiness in daily life through the powers of one's own body and mind. There is nothing in the universe which is not for a person's use. If we plant a seed, it will produce fruit two hundred and three hundred times over. The trees in the heart of the mountains grow even when they are not cultivated. The winds turn water mills. The seas carry cargoes of men and goods. Heavy boats or other vehicles can be propelled by the power of coal dug from the mountains, and by the power of water drawn from the rivers or seas to produce steam. Innumerable other things can be made with the creative forces of nature, if they are skillfully employed. Humans thus benefit by only slightly rechanneling the creative forces of nature. We add only one percent to the ninety-nine percent of resources already supplied by the hand of nature. Therefore we cannot say that we create our daily necessities; it is rather as if we pick them up strewn along the roadside. Since it is not difficult to provide them for ourselves, we cannot as men boast of being able to do it.

Of course, an independent livelihood is of the greatest importance for an individual. The ancients teach us that we should eat our bread by the sweat of our brows. But my view is that even if we do so, we have still not fulfilled our destiny as human beings. This teaching only barely raises us up to the level of the birds and the beasts. Look! Every animal provides for itself. Not only do they satisfy momentary needs; certain species, like ants, plan for their distant future by digging holes to make their nests, and by storing up food for the winter. Indeed, there are people in the world who are satisfied with doing the work of ants.

Let me give an example. A person grows up to become an artisan, a merchant, or a government official. He gradually outgrows his dependence on relatives or friends. He makes a reasonable living, without being in debt to anyone. He readily builds a simple house, or rents one. Before it is completely furnished and stocked, he marries a young woman according to his wish. He settles down to a frugal life in which his many children receive an ordinary education. He always has a fund of thirty or forty yen in readiness for emergency and illness; he is anxious about planning to live a long and frugal life. At any rate, because he has the means to secure his household, he becomes proud of the fact that he has been able to earn an independent livelihood. And society also looks up to him as an independent and free man who has achieved some great thing. But this is in fact a great mistake. This kind of individual is only a pupil of the ant. His life's work goes no further than that. He may have worked or built his house with sweat on his forehead or anxiety in his heart. There may be nothing he could be ashamed of in the light of the teachings of the ancients. But despite his success, we cannot say that he has fulfilled the end of a human being as the highest of all creation.

If a person could thus be satisfied with the mere acquisition of the necessities of life, life would mean only to be born into the world and to die: his condition at death would be no different than at his birth. If such a condition were transmitted to his children and grandchildren, a village would be eternally the same. No one would ever initiate public projects, or build boats and bridges. People would leave everything to nature except for immediate personal and family matters, with the result that there would be no trace of productive human activity anywhere.

There is a saying in the West to the effect that if men were only content with small accomplishments, there would have been no progress since the beginning of the world. This is indeed true. Of course, there are different kinds of satisfactions, which we must distinguish correctly. A person with an unsatiable desire to acquire more and more is guilty of greed or avarice. But a person who does not broaden his mental and physical powers to achieve his aims may be called ignorant and foolish.

Secondly, humans are by nature social. Hardly anything can be done in complete isolation. Human nature is not yet satisfied by the circle of spouse, parents, and children. Individuals must have wider human associations in the community. The wider their associations, the more people feel fulfillment, and this is the reason that human intercourse begins. And with community life there naturally comes attendant responsibilities. What we call learning, industry, politics, law—these are all aimed at promoting social intercourse among us. Without social intercourse they lose their meaning. Why does the government make laws? It makes laws for the precise purpose of protecting the good people from the bad, thereby making human association possible. Why do scholars write books and educate others? It is for the precise purpose of guiding the younger generation to be able to maintain human associations.

In ancient China it was said that ruling the country should be as impartial as dividing meat among people. It was also said that it was better to clean up the country than to remove weeds in the garden. These sayings describe the intentions of men who would endeavor to benefit human intercourse. A person should use his wealth to contribute to the general welfare. This is a constant principle of human nature. Even when a person does not consciously work for society, his descendants sometimes unconsciously benefit from him. It is because we humans are social by nature that we can fulfill our social obligations. If ancient people had not been such, we would not have the present advantages of civilization that we now enjoy. When a person inherits his parents' property, it is called a legacy. But this legacy merely includes a patch of land and household furnishings. They can be lost without trace. But the world's civilization is a legacy of a different sort. Each and every person receives a legacy from the human race as a whole. It is so tremendous that it cannot even be compared with land and household furnishings. But who is there to thank for these blessings? It is like receiving the sunlight and the air, so indispensable for life, without cost. For all its value, we present owners should say that civilization is entirely due to the blessings secretly bestowed by our ancestors.

In the dawn of history men's intellects were not yet developed, just like infants. For example, ancient wheat harvests were turned into flour by being pounded with natural stones. Later, through someone's invention, two stones were made flat and round, with a small hole in the center of each. An axle of wood or metal was placed through one of the holes, and over this stone the other stone was placed. This let the axle of the lower stone pass through the hole of the upper stone. The wheat was placed between the stones and ground into flour as the heavy upper stone was turned around. This is what is called a millstone. In ancient times such a millstone was turned by hand, but in later ages its shape was gradually improved. More convenient methods, such as water wheels or wind wheels, were devised, and finally steam power was used.

This is true with everything else. The world improves by a gradual evolution, so that yesterday's advanced methods are soon old-fashioned. Last year's bright new ideas are commonplace by this year. Looking at the trend towards rapid progress in Western countries, we see that as soon as the telegram, steam power, and all sorts of instruments appear, they are transformed into more and more novel forms. And it is not only the material instruments that are novel. The more our knowledge develops, the wider our social intercourse becomes. And as our associations broaden, the closer become the bonds between us. One country cannot rashly wage war against another, for the rights of nations are guaranteed under international law. There will be a gradual and unlimited advance of civilization if there can be open economic discussions, radical transformation of political and business institutions, reformation of the school systems, the forms of books, government conferences, the debates of Diet members, etc. Take the history of any Western civilization and read about it from its beginning up to the 1600s. Then skip the next two hundred years, and pick up the story again from around 1800. So astonishing will have been the leap forward in that country's progress that we can hardly believe that it is the official history of the same country. Inquiring further into the cause of its progress, we will find that it has been due to the legacy and gifts of those who went before them.

Japanese civilization, too, first came from Korea and China. Japan's civilization then progressed to its present level through our own countrymen's indefatigable efforts. As for Western Learning in Japan, it began as far back as the Hōreki Period [1751–64]. (See the woodblock print book called *Rangaku kotohajime*.)† In recent years intercourse with the foreigners began and, along with it, Western theories have been introduced to our people. Some of us Japanese have begun to teach Western learning and to translate Western works. There has been an increasing intellectual revolution; along with it, political institutions have been renovated, and the feudal domains have been dismantled. At this present moment we are again making a new start in the direction of advanced civilization. We may say that this too is the legacy of the ancients, and the gifts of those who have blazed the trail before us.

I have said above that since ancient times there have been not a few people who through their physical and mental labors contributed to the good of the world. These persons were not satisfied with their own material wealth. They valued their social responsibilities, and set their sights on doing something noble. We present-day scholars have also received a civilized legacy from these people. Since we stand in the vanguard of modern progress, there should be no limits to our way ahead. Let future generations look back upon us to thank us for our legacy to them, just as we are grateful for the blessings of the past.

Generally speaking, our entire duty lies in living in this world today in such a way as to transmit the traces of our activities to our far-distant descendants. This is a grave responsibility. We cannot be satisfied with merely reading volumes of school texts, becoming businessmen, artisans, or minor officials, just for the sake of several-hundred-yen

---

† [*Rangaku kotohajime* (Dawn of Western Science in Japan, 1815) was written by Sugita Genpaku (1733–1817), a physician of Dutch medicine. He recollects the difficulties he and his colleagues experienced when translating the Dutch anatomical table *Ontleedkundige Tafelen* into *Kaitai shinsho* (New Book on Anatomy, 1774).]

salaries so as barely to be able to support our own families. This level of activity does others no harm, but it does them no good either. Moreover, one must act in a timely way. Even a capable person cannot exercise his power if he does not act at the right times. There have been numerous examples in all ages. In my own home town I knew of talented and noble men. They may have taken wrong courses from the standpoint of modern civilization. But this was due to the conditions of their times, not to their personal faults. They could have made a contribution, for they were full of ambition to do things, but they never had the opportunity to do so. They therefore carried their treasures within themselves and took them to the grave. They were never able to give expression to their natural endowments and benefit the world. This was indeed regrettable.

But now times have changed. Western ideas have gradually come into use; the old regime has been overthrown, and the feudal domains dissolved. This should not be looked upon merely as the result of a military upheaval. The merits of civilization do not end with an ephemeral war. The real change has been a revolution in the public mind, stimulated by modern civilization. The upheaval of war has already ended seven years ago. Its traces are no longer to be seen, but the effect on public feeling continues on. Generally speaking, things cannot be guided unless they are moving. We must avail ourselves of the opportunity of the present moment to encourage learning and guide the public mind to higher levels of civilization. Since it is precisely we scholars who at the present time are presented with this opportunity, we must work very hard to accomplish this result for society.

Section
TEN

LETTER TO OLD FRIENDS IN NAKATSU, *CONTINUED*

In the former section, my argument divided the meaning of learning into two aspects. To generalize that argument, we cannot be satisfied with providing only for ourselves and our immediate families. There are higher bonds than this in human nature. Therefore we must enter into communities of social life, and work for the good of society according to our capacity as one of its members. And we must elevate our ambition to pursue learning. Even cooking rice and lighting the fire under the bath are kinds of learning. Discourse on the affairs of state is another. Still, management of a single household is easier than the economics of the whole nation.

As a rule, things which are easy to obtain are not highly valued in society. The reason why some things are valuable is that they are not easily obtainable. It seems to me that present-day scholars exhibit the vice of avoiding the difficult in favor of the easy path. In the feudal world, no matter how accomplished some scholars might have been, there was no way of putting their learning into practice, for the economy was rigid everywhere. Therefore, they were compelled to pursue more and more advanced learning. Their style of learning may not have been good, but their diligence and broad knowledge were superior to that of the scholars of today. Today's scholars are different. They can cash in quickly on what they know. For example, if a scholar of Western Learning studies for three years, he acquires a general sort of knowledge of history and physics, sufficient to open up a school as a scholar of Western Learning, to be hired by others to teach, or be given some important post in the government. And there is an even easier path than these. If they read the current popular translations, or race off to learn the latest news in society, both domestic and foreign, and then grasp the opportunity to become government officials, they become prestigious public servants! If such customs become the rule, learning will ultimately not advance to a high level.

I know that I should not write about vulgar things to scholars, but let me give an example in terms of money management. For one to study in a school, his expenses will not exceed one hundred yen a year. Thus if he invests three hundred yen for three years to get training as a scholar of Western Learning, he can later gain a profit of fifty or seventy yen per month. Since a person who just learns by experience, and then becomes a government official does not even make this three hundred yen investment, his monthly gain will all be net profit. Is there such great profit in the business world? Even a usurer cannot compete with this rate of gain. Of course, since the price of things depends on supply and demand, and nowadays the government and all other quarters are clamoring for such scholars of Western Learning, this favorable business climate has resulted. Therefore we cannot positively brand these men as crafty businessmen. Nor are we criticizing those who hire them as fools. But, in my opinion, if these men were truly made to work at practical learning through three to five additional years of grueling studies, and only thereafter given appointments, they might achieve something very fine. And only by elevating the intellectual and moral levels of the whole nation in this exacting way will we reach the point of being able to compete with the civilizations of various Western countries.

What, then, should be the goals of scholars today? Does it not lie in seeking the great principles of freedom and independence and in reviving the rights of self-autonomy and freedom? And freedom and independence already entail responsibilities. Independence does not consist exclusively in dwelling in one's own house and not depending on others for food and clothes. This is merely a domestic responsibility. We can be said to have fulfilled both our internal and external obligations only if we do not bring disgrace upon the name of

Japanese citizens, and if we strive together with our countrymen to secure the free and independent status of Japan as a world nation. Therefore, a person who barely provides for his own food and clothing within his own house may be called the independent master of his own house, but not an independent Japanese citizen.

Look around! When we survey the contemporary scene, we see the external traces of civilization, but not its inner substance. There are the outward forms, but not the inner spirit. Can we now pit our army and navy against the arms of the West? No way! Can we now teach the West with our techniques of scholarship? We have nothing to teach them. On the contrary, we must learn these things from abroad, fearing only that we have not yet reached their levels. We send students abroad, but when it comes to hiring teachers in Japan, they are generally all foreigners, from government offices and schools down to the prefectures and the ports. Even private companies and schools, when they plan some new undertaking, must first hire foreigners and rely on them at the cost of excessive salaries. People say that Japan is just using their talents to make up for our deficiencies. But if we look at present conditions, it seems that the deficiencies are all on our side, and the talents all on theirs.

Of course, since we have just suddenly begun intercourse with the civilized nations after several hundred years of national seclusion, our situation is like mixing fire and water. To balance this relationship, foreign teachers and goods are being imported to make up for present urgent needs and calm down the seething turmoil. Since it is unavoidable anyhow, dependence on these temporary supplies cannot be said to be an error for Japan.

Nevertheless, meeting the needs of Japan by depending on the West is only a temporary policy. While we may comfort ourselves that it is a temporary expediency, when will this come to an end? How will methods be acquired so that we will be independent of the West and can supply our own needs? They will be extremely hard to come by.

Our only recourse is to wait for the achievements of today's scholars to reach a point where they can meet Japan's needs. Since this is the duty imposed upon us scholars it is high time to take on this urgent responsibility. In the short run the foreigners employed within

Japan must retain their posts as substitutes until our own scholars are mature. Foreign goods must also be temporarily imported in exchange for cash until Japan's own industries are sufficiently developed. The funds spent to import men and goods from abroad is money lost to the foreigners since Japanese scholarship is not yet on a par with theirs. We should regret this for the sake of the nation, and as scholars we should have a sense of shame. But, as persons, we can still have high hopes for the future. Without hopes, nothing can be accomplished in life. We should therefore comfort ourselves during the present misfortune by looking to tomorrow's potential blessings. We must endure this year's suffering by looking to next year's happiness.

In former times, all the areas of life were constrained by the ancient system, so that even a scholar with a will had no scope to fulfill his ambitions. Today it is different. Now that restrictions have been removed, a new world is opening up before scholars. There is no area in society to which we cannot devote our energies. There are hundreds of things to be done—farming, business, scholarship, government life, writing books, writing for newspapers, giving lectures on law, developing the techniques of learning and arts, starting up industries, opening the Diet chambers, etc. Moreover, our motive need not be mutual struggle between brothers, but intellectual competition with the West. If we are victorious in this battle, Japan's position will be enhanced; if vanquished, her prestige will decline. Our hopes must be high, and our aims clear. Of course, the priorities of the affairs of the nation will vary with conditions. But from now on people must begin to use their talents to study the absolutely indispensable things. People who realize their social obligations to any degree must not stand by as indifferent onlookers in today's world. We scholars must especially apply all efforts.

Given this perspective, we scholars can hardly be satisfied with elementary and secondary school education. We must elevate our sights to appreciate the true worth of learning. We must be autonomous and independent. If we have no friends of kindred minds, we should cultivate our spirit alone to preserve Japan, and thereby devote our efforts for the sake of society. I do not cherish the fact that old-style scholars of Japanese and Chinese Learning know how to govern others, but not how to govern themselves. Precisely because I do not, I advocated the doctrine of the equal rights of man from the beginning of this work, and have been discussing the position that persons must take responsibility for their own affairs, and the importance of relying on their own power. But in regard to this matter of providing for oneself, I have not exhausted this topic of the significance of learning. If you have a dissolute and profligate youth, what kind of discipline would you employ to control him? To make a man out of him, his drinking and playboy life must first be prohibited before he can be given a post of any importance. But we cannot call it virtue simply because he has put off these vices. He has stopped doing harm to society, but he is still a useless fellow. Only after stopping these vices, taking on some job, cultivating his person, and bringing profit to his household can he be called an average fellow.

The same argument applies to providing only for oneself. Persons from the samurai families and above have been accustomed to the old ways for thousands of years. They do not know the value of clothing and food. Having no idea of how wealth is acquired, they haughtily, and without efforts on their own part, are well provided for, and they think that it is their natural privilege as well. Their condition is generally like the dissolute son. What can I say to such people? I can only advocate my doctrine of providing for oneself to shake them out of their drunken dreams. Should I try to exhort them to pursue learning of a high level? Should I explain to them the great principle of contributing to society? Even if I tried to, since it would enter within their knowledge in their present dream-like state, it would only be a dream within a dream. This is the reason why I chiefly advocate the doctrine of providing for oneself, and do not urge true learning on them.

Accordingly, this doctrine of mine was aimed mainly at those who lead lives of idleness. It was not an admonition to scholars. But I hear that among my old friends in Nakatsu, some persons who pursued a career of learning have gone only halfway and then given it up to make their livelihood. Making a livelihood must also not be belittled, of course. I can approve of the fact that they are deciding their future course of life on the basis of their own talents. But I fear that if people imitate such customs and only compete for livelihood, their fine promise as brilliant youths will fail to bear full fruit. This is regrettable for both the boys and the nation as well. Livelihood is difficult to come by, but if they plan the management of their households well, it is better to expend their efforts, and be frugal, while looking for an opportunity for great accomplishment, than to earn money quickly to buy minor happiness. If they pursue careers as scholars, they must study to the utmost. If they become merchants or farmers, let them be great ones; similarly, if they become scholars, let them not be satisfied with small achievements. Let them not be deterred by heat or cold, by coarse clothes and poor foods; let them pound rice and cut wood—they can pursue learning even as they pound rice! Moreover, their foods are not limited to Western-style menus. Let them pursue the matters of civilization while they eat boiled barley and drink *miso* soup!

Section
ELEVEN

THE FALSITY OF THE IDEA OF MORAL SUBORDINATION

In section Eight I gave examples of harm done to women and children through the concept of the moral subordination of inferiors to superiors. I noted many such abuses that extend even outside of the family. To take up, in the first place, the origin of this theory, its form certainly is reducible to the principle of might makes right. But it does not necessarily arise from evil intentions. It consists rather in regarding people as ignorant and good people who are easy to control, i.e. who should be succored and guided by their total subservience to the commands of their superiors who are to handle all matters according to their own discretion. The minds of superiors and inferiors are supposed to be in perfect accord on the national level, the village level, or in a shop or household. All human relations are to be treated after the parent-child relation. For example, in dealing with children of about ten years of age, they should not, of course, be allowed to decide things for themselves. They should be clothed and fed according to the judgments of their parents. Only if their children are obedient should they have warm clothing in cold weather and good food when hungry. Food and clothing will then be in abundance as if rained down from heaven. The children will have these things when they need them, and thus live with complete freedom and security of mind. Since parents love their children even more than themselves, the instructions and discipline, encouragements and scoldings which they give their children will spring from loving affection. The relation between parents and children will be very close, and their joy will be beyond compare. In other terms, their union will fulfill the moral relationship that is quite appropriate to this case.

Now, the advocates of the theory of moral subordination make an interesting case for extending the parent-child relation to all human relations. But there are grave objections to this. The parent-child relation can only be one between real parents, whose wisdom is mature, and their own immature children. It is impossible for the same relation to prevail with another person's child. Again, when their own child grows up to over twenty years of age, the parents must change their attitudes towards the child. Still more is this so in the case between adult strangers. It is impossible that this latter relationship be based on the same principle. It is what is called "easier said than done." Indeed, nation, village, government, or business companies are all relations among grown-ups and among strangers. Will it not be difficult to apply the principle of parent-child relationship here? Yet, however difficult it might be, the fancy that it would be extremely good to try seems to be a constant propensity of human nature. This is the reason why the theory of moral obligations based on the parent-child relation emerges in society, and the reason why tyranny has subsequently been practiced. Therefore, I say that the source of the idea of stratified moral relationships does not necessarily derive from evil intentions, but has perforce been the product of such fancies.

In the countries of Asia, the monarch has been called the parent of the people, the people have been called his subjects and children. The work of the government has been called the office of shepherd of the masses, and in China local officials were called the shepherds of such-and-such provinces. Since this word *boku*† means to feed animals, it had the connotation of treating the people of single provinces as cows or sheep, and that name was publicly written on the notice boards. Was this not an extremely discourteous way of saying and doing things? But even though they treated their citizens as children or barn animals, the word originally did not necessarily have such an evil meaning. It had something like the idea of the care of children by their parents.

---

† [The word Fukuzawa is referring to is *boku* 牧, which literally means "shepherd."]

First, the monarch was described as a sage and enlightened man; then, wise and virtuous officials were employed to assist him. These leaders were without any selfishness of mind or the slightest personal desires. They were pure as water, and straightminded as an arrow. They extended their own affection to the people, whom they cherished and loved. In times of famine they gave them food; in the event of fires they gave them money. Thus they relieved them in their sufferings, so that the people could enjoy peace and comfort in their daily lives. The moral influence of the superior class was as redolent as the fragrance which the south wind brings. The people, in turn, submitted like the grasses bending in the breeze. Or their docility was like soft cotton. Their innocence was like wood and stones. Superiors and inferiors could then sing of the great harmony in perfect unison. All this was the original intention of the theory. Indeed, it was an imitation of the conditions of paradise.

Nevertheless, if we consider the facts more deeply, the relation between government and people is not that of flesh and blood. It is in essence an association of strangers. Personal feelings cannot be the guiding principle in an association among strangers. It is necessarily based on the creation of a social rule and social contract. Even when they dispute over minute points of interpretation, if both of them abide by the rule, they will come to some peaceful agreement. And for this reason national laws are created. It may be essential to have the above hierarchy of enlightened monarch, excellent ministers, and docile people, but by entering what schools can such faultless sages be created? By what educational process can such splendid citizens be obtained?

The Chinese have in fact been concerned with these ideas since the Zhou dynasty. But from the Zhou to the present there never has been a time of peace and good government based on those essential ingredients. Has not the upshot been that China has been oppressed by foreigners, as witnessed again today? Not seeming to learn the significance of this, they are like persons who swallow the same inefficacious medicines over and over again. They employ an extremely artificial concept of "benevolent government." These sages, who were not divine, would endeavor to blend injustice with benevolent government, and thus force blessings upon the people. But when blessings turn into burdens, and virtuous rule changes into harsh laws, do they still sing of the great harmony? If they desire to sing, let them sing alone. No one will join them any more. For their original intention was itself too wide of the mark. China may be our close neighbor, but her situation is unendurably ridiculous.

This kind of behavior has not been limited to the relation with the government. It is universal—in merchant houses, schools, shrines and temples. Let me give just one example. In a business shop, the master is supposed to be the expert in all things. He alone handles the ledger. Then there are the clerks and assistants, who, while concentrating on their own tasks, do not know the management of the whole business. They only do the will of their noisy and blustering boss, who dictates their salary and their tasks. They cannot tell how the business is going from looking in the ledger. Day and night they just look at their master's expressions. They can only surmise that the business is going well if he is cheerful, or suppose it is not when he is gloomy. They themselves have no other cares, except secretly to manipulate the books which they have charge of in order to embezzle funds. Even the eagle-eyed boss does not catch what is going on. Although he thought that a certain servant† was completely trustworthy, when the records are checked after he absconds or suddenly dies, the books show that he has gouged out a hole of embezzled money as big as a cave. Only then does the master of the shop sigh over how untrustworthy men are. But the cause does not lie there. It comes from his own original despotism over all things. Since he and the servant were adults who were completely unrelated to one another, the cause of the trouble can be said to have been due to his own indiscretion of not promising a fairer share of the business to him, whom he in fact treated like a child.

This kind of poisonous atmosphere creates the sick condition of swindling and subterfuge prevalent among men because of the above stress on moral subservience practiced in an exclusive and tyrannical way. I call people who are infected with this sickness "pseudo

---

† The name Chūsuke 忠助 is used, playing on the literal meaning of "loyal servant."

gentlemen." In the feudal age, for example, the retainers of a daimyo were all on the surface loyal retainers. In outward form, they were true to those moral relations between superiors and inferiors. They performed every act of deference to their lord and kept their prescribed distances when bowing. At the anniversary of his death they observed abstinence. At the birthday of a young lord they wore ceremonial dress. At the New Year observances and visits to the grave of his ancestors, no one was absent. According to their own way of saying it, "poverty was the constant way of the warrior," or "loyalty and patriotism," or "sacrifice one's life for one's lord." They made such statements of great dedication that in times of crisis they would have the spirit to rush off to die in battle. Ordinary people may have been taken in by all this, but if we quietly consider it from another point of view, they were, as might be expected, pseudo gentlemen.

For if there was a retainer of a daimyo who discharged his office well, why was it that his family became rich? With a fixed hereditary stipend and wages for his office, there was no reason for him to have even one sen of extra income. It was therefore very strange that he should have money left over after balancing out income and expenses. It was certain that he had cheated his lord out of his money, whether through perquisite or bribery. I will give some conspicuous examples of this, as follows. It seems to have been almost a regular rule in the families of the three hundred feudal lords that the head official in charge of construction would demand a kick-back from the carpenters; and the finance officials took presents from the townsmen under their patronage. Was it not extremely improper for loyal retainers who had pledged even to die for their lord by risking their lives in front of his horse to take commissions for buying things? They should be called pseudo gentlemen plated superficially with gold. Some rare honest official might gain a reputation in the domain as an honorable retainer *par excellence* for being above bribery. But he was in fact only doing his job without stealing. It was no cause for praise just because he had not set his heart on robbery. He who was an ordinary person stood out only by contrast with the rest, who were the pseudo gentlemen. In the last analysis, the cause of the abundance of those pseudo gentlemen was the ancient wild fancy that the people of the land were all docile and easily controlled. This error finally led to despotism and oppression. The dog ultimately bit his master's hand. Indeed, the theory of moral subservience is the most unreliable one in the whole world, just as the worst poisons are despotism and suppression. They are indeed horrible.

Some may say that the examples of evil people's insincerity are limitless, but not all people are like this—Japan has been a just country, in which from ancient times there have been many examples of loyal retainers who have given their lives for their lords. To this I answer that so it was. We have not been without examples of loyal retainers since ancient times. But their number has been so small that the accounts do not tally. The Genroku Period, for example, can be called the period when the flower of chivalry was in full bloom. At that time there were forty-seven loyal samurai in the Akō clan with its 70,000 *koku* income. In a domain of 70,000 *koku* there were about 70,000 people. If there were forty-seven in 70,000 there should have been about 4,700 in seven million. But chivalry also declined with the changing of the seasons of history, as people also say, and truly, too. Therefore deducting thirty percent from the supposed chivalry of the Genroku Period, for seven million people the proportion should be about 70% of 4,700, which is 3,290. If the present population of Japan is about thirty million, the number of loyal people should be 14,100. A child of three can calculate that this number is not enough to protect present-day Japan.

According to my above arguments, the concept of moral subservience has been an utter failure. Let me say a few more words on the subject. *Meibun*,† or the theory of moral subservience, is an empty concept, and the concepts of "high" and "low," and "noble" and "base" are equally useless. Now if these ostentatious names and the actual responsibilities truly corresponded, and people really fulfilled their duties, I do not think I would have any objection to them. That is, the government is the country's counting room, and has the duty to rule the people. The people are the country's financiers, and have the duty financially to support the government. The duty of civil officials is

---

† *Meibun* 名分 is a Confucian idea of moral obligation according to one's "name" or station.

to confer and decide upon the laws of the government. The duty of military officers is to go out and fight according to their commands. In addition, there are set duties for scholars and townsmen. But if an upstart of superficial learning hears that his duties were unnecessary and forgets them, or breaks the law as a citizen; or if the government meddles with private industry; or if soldiers discuss politics and start wars on their own; or if civil officials submit to brute force and obey the command of military officers—if such things were to happen, the country would be in great turmoil. There would be anarchy and lawlessness, caused by superficial knowledge of independence and freedom. *Meibun* or "moral subservience" and *shokubun*[†] or "one's duty" may look alike in written characters, but they are completely different in meaning. Scholars should not misunderstand this distinction.

---

† The original Chinese character *shokubun* 職分 literally means "one's (professional) duty." Fukuzawa also discusses it in the Section Four, "The Duty of Scholars," and Section Seven, "The Duties of the Citizens of the Nation."

Section
TWELVE

AN ENCOURAGEMENT OF PUBLIC SPEAKING

Enzetsu is called "speech" in English. It is a style of expressing one's views at a large assembly of people. This kind of thing has since ancient times never existed in Japan, except perhaps for preaching done in temples. But it is very popular in the West. From the parliament of a government, the meetings of scholars, business companies, and gatherings of citizens, down to ceremonial occasions and even trivial matters such as the opening of a shop, there is a custom that whenever there is a gathering of ten or more people, some person always makes a speech about the meeting or the purpose of the meeting, or utters some pet theory, or expresses some impromptu ideas. It is beyond doubt that this is a very important practice. For example, people are now saying that Japan should have a parliament.† But it will serve no purpose unless there is a method of expounding ideas in the first place.

Setting aside the question of whether a given subject is important or not, one who expresses his views through public speaking can produce a certain good effect. For example, something which was not so significant in a written text can become easily understood and impressive if said in words. This is true of famous poems from ancient and modern times. If put in ordinary prose form, these poems would lose their interest. But when they are well structured according to the rules of

---

† [At the time Fukuzawa was writing *An Encouragement of Learning*, arguments in favor of the establishment of the Japanese parliament were gaining momentum. Itagaki Taisuke (1837–1919) initiated the debate when he presented a petition for representative government in 1874.]

poetry, they become extremely charming and moving. In like manner, the rapid transmission of one's ideas to the public has a great deal to do with the method of its transmission.

It is not necessary to reiterate here that learning does not consist only in the reading of books. The essence of learning lies rather in its practical consequences, without which learning is still ignorance. In the past, there was a student of Chu Hsi philosophy who studied for many years in Edo, copying out theories of the different masters on the schools of learning. By his long, day-and-night labors he piled up several hundred volumes in several years' time. Having thus completed his studies, he decided to return to his home in the west along the Tōkaidō. He therefore packed up his copied books in arrowroot baskets, and shipped them on ahead. But unfortunately the ship was wrecked in the Sea of Enshū. When he returned to his native province, he found out that all his learning had been washed away with the waves. He was back exactly where he started, in a state of total ignorance. The same danger exists for the present crop of Japanese scholars of Western learning. Because they now read and lecture in the city schools, we cannot help calling them scholars. But if circumstances suddenly took away their sources and forced them back to the rural areas, they might have to make the excuse to their relatives and friends: "I have left my learning back in Tokyo."

My point is that the essence of learning lies in the activity of one's mind, not in the mere reading of books. There must be all kinds of means to put this activity to practical use. The word **observation** means the perceiving of things, and **reasoning** means the inferring of the principles of things and giving one's own views on the matter. But neither exhausts the methods of learning. It is also necessary to read and write books, converse with others, and present your opinions to the public. A person may be called a true scholar only when he has made use of all these means. Observation, reasoning, and reading are the means through which knowledge is gathered; conversation the means of its exchange; reading and public speaking the means of the diffusion of learning. Some of these a person can do by himself, but conversation and public speaking require a larger community. From this we can see how important public speaking is.

The most lamentable thing about the Japanese people today is that their views are not lofty. Therefore, since it is the first duty of scholars to guide them to higher views, they must avail themselves of whatever means they can command for doing so. It is demonstrable that conversation and public speaking are essential to the pursuit of learning, but why then do people not actually use them? It is because of the indolence of scholars. Human affairs have both private and public aspects, and both of them are necessary. But many scholars are exclusively absorbed in private matters. A true scholar must, when alone, be as silent as deep water, but among people he must be as active as a flying bird; he must be deeply introspective, yet at the same time have a boundless public energy—only then can he call himself a true scholar.

THE REFINEMENT OF CONDUCT

To repeat, the most lamentable thing about the Japanese people today is that their views are not lofty. The refinement of one's views and conduct cannot be achieved merely by studying lofty principles. The Zen sect preaches a way of spiritual enlightenment, the principle of which is said to be very recondite. But as we look at the monks' activities, we see that they are so remote as to be of no practical use. In fact, their ideas are vague to the point of being no opinions at all.

Again, one's views and conduct must not be lofty only in the breadth of experience. There are people who do not possess definite views of their own despite reading thousands of books and a wider association with others. They are the Confucian scholars who cling to old customs. Even the scholars of Western learning are not exceptional, being addicted to the same vice. There are people today who follow the ever advancing learning of the West. They read books on economics, or lecture on moral theories, or concentrate their energies night and day on metaphysics and epistemology—almost as if their hard effort were comparable to the pain one suffers from sitting atop bristling thorns. But as far as I can see, the private lives of these people give no evidence of the effects of all this effort. Their knowledge of economics has no influence on their family business. Their knowledge of moral theories has no bearing on their own moral cultivation. As talkers and doers they seem to be two entirely different persons. I cannot find anyone with his own definite views. Even if we do not go so far as to condemn their words and actions as wrong, there is a complete discrepancy between what they say is right and what they actually practice. They sometimes practice what they preach, but to them can often be applied the sayings that "A physician neglects his own health," and "Some people can read the *Analects* of Confucius but do not understand it."

Therefore lofty opinions and conduct refer neither to expounding profound principles nor to breadth of knowledge taken in an exclusive sense. How, then, can a person's views be elevated to influence his conduct? The secret lies in comparing the conditions of things and setting one's sights on higher standards without ever becoming complacent. But this means to compare, not single details, but one total system of conditions with another, and to pass judgment on the relative merits of the alternatives. Suppose that there is a schoolboy who has worked hard, without indulging in dissolute pleasures. He will not be reproached by his parents or elders, and most likely feels proud of himself. But he has reason for pride only in comparison with some other rascals. Diligence and good behavior are what were expected of him, and are not worthy of special praise. He should have even nobler aspirations in life.

Whose great achievements, and whom should we strive to emulate, among the great men of the past and present? We must always take persons of higher attainment as our standards. We should not be satisfied with our own one talent when we see two talents in another. This is true since later progress will inevitably surpass earlier progress, and this is all the more true when there is no one worth emulating in the past. Today's responsibilities are greater than those in the past. However, we cannot think that diligence and good conduct are the sole aims of human life. A life of dissolution is animal; to pride oneself in comparison with that would merely be boasting of one's sight before a blind man. It would only be a useless display of stupidity. Therefore an argument is still on a low level if it is about the pros and cons of dissolute conduct. As one's conduct improves, he will soon leave such stupid talk behind him, so that even discussion of the matter will become detestable.

In their criticism of schools today, parents are solely concerned with the control of public morals. But what does the phrase "public morals" mean? It must mean strict observance of school regulations and thorough discipline over the student's moral life. Should we praise these things as ideal for an academic institution? On the contrary, I am ashamed of them. Public morals in Western schools are by no means all good. Many of them, on the contrary, are very bad. But I have never heard of a reputation of a school being based on correct morals and thorough control of discipline.

The reputation of a school depends only on the excellent quality of the subjects of study, the skill of the teachers, their level of refinement, and the high quality of their discussions. Therefore, both administrators and students should not compare their schools with inferior schools, but with schools of finer quality. The moral conduct and discipline of a school may be counted among its merits, but this is the least important aspect of a school, and not worth boasting about. They should make even greater efforts if they want to compare favorably with schools of higher academic quality. Accordingly, while we are pressed with the management of a school, we should not be satsified merely if the control is well organized.

The same principle can be applied to the conditions of a country. Suppose that a given administration is run by wise, virtuous, and irreproachable men. Since they understand the joys and sorrows of the people, they take proper measures to reward the meritorious and punished the wicked. They command both mercy and severity. The people are well supplied and enjoy the fruits of peace. But rewards and punishments, mercy and severity, peace and prosperity are all domestic affairs under the control of one or only a handful of administrators. They can have reason to take pride only in comparison of present conditions with some former administration or some evil government. This is hardly to make a detailed and thoroughgoing comparison with another country. If one nation as a whole is compared with another civilized country over several decades, it may be that the relative accomplishments of one nation will not be worth especially boasting about.

Take, for example, the national polity of India, the origin of whose civilization dates back several thousand years. The subtlety and abstruseness of its philosophies are probably not inferior to the philosophies of the modern West. The ancient Turkish government, too, was most prestigious. In ritual, music, the arts of war, there was nothing that was not well organized. The rulers were wise; court officials were irreproachable. Its teeming population and brave soldiers were superior to its neighboring countries, so that for a while it won universal fame. Therefore, if we make comments on India or Turkey, we must say that the former was once a famous center of culture and the latter was a great military empire.

Yet India is now a colony of Great Britain, and her people are no different than slaves of the British government. Their only business is to produce opium to poison the Chinese, while the British merchants reap the profits from the opium trade. Turkey too, while nominally independent, has become a monopoly of British and French business interests. Its national products decline day by day, as a result of the free trade. Its people no longer weave cloth or make looms. Either they cultivate the land with sweat on their brows, or they loaf about idly all day. They rely entirely upon British and French imports for all manufactured articles. There are no means to manage the economy of the country, and it is said that no matter how brave her soldiers may be, they are of no use because they are restrained by poverty.

Now, why is it that Indian culture and Turkish military heritage have not benefited the civilizations of each? The reason is that the minds of their peoples were turned complacently in on themselves. When they compared themselves with other nations, they took only a partial look, and were thus deceived by the seeming balance of potentials between nations. So their discussions ended there. They did not compare themselves with another country's total resources and conditions. Therefore while their people enjoyed peace or quarreled domestically, other nations passed them by, and then came to oppress them with the power of modern commerce. The merchants of the West were without rivals wherever they went. They are certainly to be feared for their business prowess. But if people love their own civilization, they should strive to the best of their powers to catch up with them in every respect.

Section
THIRTEEN

THE DAMAGE OF ENVY IN SOCIETY

Of the many human vices, none is more damaging to society than envy. Greed, luxury, and defamation are other notable vices, but properly considered, they are not vices in the quality of the actions themselves. Circumstances sometimes neutralize them as vices, i.e. their degree and purpose are contributing factors. For example, greed is an insatiable love of money, but love of money is a part of human nature. They can hardly be blamed if a person satisfies this love in accordance with human nature. Only if he mistakes its proper place by seeking to gain money by unjust means, thereby overstepping the principle and purpose of the possession of money, can it be called the vice of greed. Therefore we cannot immediately label it a vice every time we come across a mind which appreciates money. A certain principle demarcates the borderline of virtue and vice. Those who remain within this borderline can be called frugal and economical. Indeed, such an attitude is one of the excellent virtues for which men should strive.

It is the same with luxury. It becomes a virtue or vice depending entirely on how far it goes. It is human nature to want to wear warm clothes and live in a safe house. How can it be called a vice to comfort oneself according to human nature? To accumulate and spend, but to spend without going beyond the proper limits, may also be called one of the finer virtues of man.

Again, there is hardly any difference between defamation and refutation of another. Maliciously to distort another person's statements is called defamation; to state what one thinks to be the truth by exposing another's contradictions is called refutation. Accordingly, as long as the right road of truth has not yet been found, discussions between men cannot be determined as either good or bad. Until right and wrong are determined, we may say that public opinion should serve as the truth, but it is extremely difficult to clarify just what public opinion is. Therefore we cannot immediately call it slander when we see one person attacking another. In fact, it may be necessary to seek the truth all over the world in order to distinguish whether it is slander or true refutation.

In addition to the above, arrogance and bravery, coarseness and frankness, stubbornness and steadiness, levity and sharpness are all relative opposites. They become virtues or vices only by the circumstances, degree, and purpose of each act. It is only envy which is a vice through and through in the nature of the actions, regardless of circumstance or purpose.

For envy is a completely negative thing and never has a positive side. It is a discontent with the conditions of another, demanding too much of one, without reflecting upon oneself. Such a means to gratify one's discontent does one's self no good, and harms the other as well. For example, when a person compares his own bad luck with another's good fortune while not taking the means to better his own condition, but instead downgrades the condition of the other and thereby seeks to bring the other down to his own level—this is what you might call "hating another and wishing his death." Therefore to feed this discontent only by depreciating the fortunes of others can be of no positive value at all.

Some men say that deception and lies rank with envy for being evil in essence. I reply that while this may seem to be so, they cannot be put in the same category once their causes and results are distinguished. Deception and lies are, of course, great evils, but they are rather the results than the causes of envy. Envy is, as it were, the mother of a whole brood of vices. Suspicion, jealousy, fear, cowardice are all her offspring. It appears inwardly in the forms of furtive talk, whispering, confidential remarks, secret intrigues; outwardly it assumes the destructive forms of cliques, assassinations, rebellions, civil wars. They bring not the slightest benefit to the nation. No one escapes from the trouble which they bring in their wake. They can be called promoting one's own private interests at the public expense.

Such is the damage to society caused by envy. Now to consider its causes, it lies in a kind of impasse which people get into. This is not an impasse in financial matters. It is something which drives man's natural functions to extremity by impeding human communication and enterprise. If financial distress were the cause of envy, the poor of the nation would all be complaining of injustice, the rich and noble would be the focus of their wrath, and human intercourse would not last a single day. But this is not the actual fact. Even the poorest of people, if they realize that the causes of their poverty and low station lie in themselves, do not recklessly vent their envy on others. We need not write up all the evidences as this is obvious from the fact that men maintain social relations despite the differences between rich and poor, high and low throughout the world today. Therefore I say that, in themselves, wealth and high station are not the objects of anger, nor are poverty and low station necessary causes of discontent.

Envy is accordingly not produced by poverty and low station. Rather it thrives in conditions where people's natural functions are blocked and all human fortunes are considered accidental. Confucius once sighed and said that it was difficult to deal with women and small-minded men. But now as I see it, I must say that this was a situation which Confucius himself brought about, and he himself was displaying this vice. For there is no principle in terms of which human nature can be differentiated according to sex. Again, when he spoke of small-minded men, did he mean lowly persons? The children of the lowly are not necessarily inferior, and, needless to say, there are no innate distinctions between noble and inferior. But why, then, was Confucius troubled only by women and small-minded people? This was because Confucius taught people in general to be servile. He thus lumped together the weak women and lowly people, and did not allow them any individual freedom in any of their actions at all. Thereby Confucius implanted a spirit of envy in them, and when it reached an extreme, even he had to lament about it.

When a person's nature cannot find free expression, he will inevitably become envious of others. The law of cause and effect is as clear as barley growing from barley seeds. Confucius may have had the reputation of being a sage, but he did not understand this principle. It was quite untrustworthy of him simply to complain about the stupidity of others without doing anything constructive about it. Of course, since Confucius lived in an age of barbarism and primitivism over two thousand years ago, he must have followed the custom and human sentiment of the time and knowingly resorted to the expedient of labeling people to preserve lofty public mindedness in his own day. But if Confucius had been a true sage whose wisdom provided insight for all times, he would not have been satisfied with the expedient teaching of that time. And therefore, by taking the ideas of his time into account, those who study Confucius in later times must deal with his thought selectively. Those who would apply unchanged to Meiji Japan the teachings of two thousand years ago do not know the true value of things.

Let me give an example closer to our own times. Of those who were filled with the poison of envy and did the most harm to human relations, the worst were the many ladies in the castles of the feudal lords of Japan. Generally speaking, the palaces were packed with ignorant and unlettered females who served a single ignorant and unvirtuous lord. Study went unrewarded, indolence unpunished; remonstrance produced no reaction; it was irrelevant whether one spoke out or remained silent, whether one told the truth or not. The only thing that mattered was whether they had the good luck to be in the lord's favor and affection by adapting themselves to the changing circumstances which each new day brought. It was like shooting a bow without a target; to hit or miss the target was not a matter of skill. They may be said to have lived in another world in which the nature of their emotions—delight, anger, sorrow, and pleasure—were subject to change, making them different from the rest of society. When some lady established herself in the lord's favor through her contacts, the others could only be jealous of her since there was no way to study the method by which she established herself. In the excess of their jealousy, they could only seethe with hate.

Since they were so burning with jealousy and envy, what time did they have to consider the good of the lord's house? Their loyalty and integrity were pronouncements in name only. But in actual fact, even if they spilled oil on the mat floor, if no one saw it, they would leave it there without wiping it up. Even worse, when the lord was mortally sick, they were so entangled in glaring daggers of hate at one another that many could not even care for their sick lord, even though they might have wished to. But the most vicious extreme of envy and jealousy was when it sometimes took the form of poisoning. If we had **statistics** of this crime of all times and could compare the ratios of poisonings in the castles of old and in the world, we would clearly see how much more prevalent poisoning was in the feudal castles. It would serve to prove how terrible the harm of envy is.

I think that we can infer the general condition of society even from this one example of the castle ladies. Envy is the worst of human ills. Therefore, since the causes of envy lie in a kind of spiritual impasse, the avenues of human expression must be opened. People must be given the opportunity to give free rein to their actions. Let us compare conditions in England or America with Japan. Let me pose the question: Which country, in its social relations, is most removed from the above-described situation of the feudal castles? I am not implying that Japan's situation is exactly equal to the above case, but if the point is the relative distance from it, Japan is closer to it than England or America. It is not that the English and Americans are not covetous and extravagant, or coarse and disruptive, or false and deceitful. Their manners and customs are not all good either; but when it comes to suppressing envy, they differ in mentality from the Japanese. Nowadays, intellectuals are talking about the need of a Diet elected by the people and about freedom of the press. Passing over the merits and demerits of their arguments, their basic reason lies in wanting to make Japan different from the castles of old, and to make the Japanese people different from the castle ladies. They want to replace envy with action, to put a stop to resentment by encouraging free competition, to win fame and fortune through their own efforts. They want to make the people of the whole country reap what they have sown.

The obstruction of free expression and free enterprise among the people is generally considered a political question. If someone suddenly heard talk of this question, he might ascribe it exclusively to the defects of the government. But this kind of sickness is not limited to government only. It has infected the people as well with extremely harmful results. Hence it cannot be cured only by reform of government. Let me say a few more words about this problem outside of government at the end of this section.

Human beings are by nature social animals; they can come to dislike society only through the force of habit. There are eccentric and odd persons who purposely cut themselves off from society by living in mountain villages or remote hamlets. We call them recluses. Even persons who are perhaps not true recluses may dislike being involved with the world. They make proud faces as they lock up their homes and have no intercourse with worldly affairs. Their intention does not necessarily lie in withdrawing themselves over dissatisfaction with the actions of the government. Their minds and wills are timid and weak. They do not have the courage to get involved with things. They are narrow-minded and intolerant of others. Because they do not tolerate others, others do not tolerate them either. Both sides thus step further and further backwards. Their differences become glaring, and finally they become enemies and end up hating each other. This must be said to be a great evil for society.

Again, in reference to human relations, there are people who look at another's deeds without interest in the person himself, or listen to the report of his words from a distance. When the other does not accord with their own wills, they never are sympathetic or loving; on the contrary, they nurture thoughts of dislike and disapproval. Many, in fact, go to the extreme of hate. This also is the result of human nature and habit. If people would discuss things personally more often, matters which cannot be solved through intermediaries or letters may be completely cleared up. People usually say: "Actually, this is the case. But if I have to face that person, I cannot tell him exactly what I think." In other words, there are sincere feelings of human nature which incline a person toward being tolerant. Once there is tolerance on both sides, they will understand one another, and envy will vanish away. For example, I have often said that the many assassinations of past and present times might not have happened, if there had been the opportunity for the one assassinated and his murderer to have been together for several days to express their true minds. Even such enemies might have not only made peace, but perhaps even become rare friends.

From the above consideration we can see that the obstruction of free expression and human enterprise is not merely a sickness of the government. It is prevalent among the people of the whole country. Even scholars have not avoided its contamination. The vital energies of human life cannot develop unless they are in contact with things. Let men speak and work freely, and leave fortune and social station to the persons themselves to attain, without being impeded by others.

Section
FOURTEEN

A CRITICISM OF PEOPLE'S THOUGHTS

As i observe people passing their lives, I find that they do more evil and foolish things than they think in their hearts, and do not achieve so much success as they had planned. But no matter how wicked people are, there is no one who devotes his whole life to doing only evil deeds. Yet, meeting with opportunities in the course of daily life, a person may suddenly be tempted to do evil, even though he knows quite well that it is so. He may make selfish excuses of various sorts to console himself. Or when he does some evil to another, he may not at all think that it was wrong, and so feel no shame. He may even think that he has done something good, so that when another holds a different view on the matter, he becomes angry and resentful. But as the months and years pass by and he reflects further upon his past deed, he will be filled with shame, realizing that he was in fact at great fault.

In human nature there are differences in intelligence and strength, but there are no people who think that they are inferior to the birds and beasts in intelligence. Sometimes a person chooses a task in society he thinks is suited to his own capability, but as he gets into his work he unexpectedly makes many blunders. His original estimation had been a miscalculation. He will be laughed at by people and come to regret that he ever set his blunder in motion. We onlookers may regard his miscalculation as something truly ridiculous. But the person who planned this was not necessarily so stupid. Further inquiry may show that he was indeed justified in making the attempt he did. In the busy world of men, changes of fortune are not easily predictable. Because of this, even wise men do more foolish things than they intend.

A person's prospects are always grand, and it is extremely difficult to calculate the difficulty and size of an undertaking with the length of time it will take. [Benjamin] Franklin [1706–90] once said that at first one may calculate a time-frame to be satisfactory, but as he actually attends to it, he will end up finding that it is not.[†] How true this is! When we instruct a carpenter to do some work, or order a tailor to make a suit of clothes, they will end up behind schedule eight or nine times out of ten. They do not necessarily do this out of rudeness. They simply did not make an accurate calculation regarding how long the work would take in the first place, and consequently ended up breaking their promises.

It is not uncommon for people to reproach carpenters or tailors for breaking their promises. They may offer some reason for doing so; carpenters and tailors are always coming up with excuses and the customers are always forced to be understanding. But have these gentlemen themselves ever finished promised work on schedule? After a student leaves his home in the country promising to endure every hardship to complete his course of studies in three years, does he fulfill his promise? Does the person who raised money with difficulty and bought original sources which he had longed for and promised himself to read through in three months' time ever really fulfill his intention? If a concerned public-spirited gentlemen makes a repeated petition to come into government office so to introduce sweeping reforms, etc., does he ever remain true to his word after coming into office? If a needy student says that if he had ten thousand *ryō* of gold he would build schools tomorrow throughout the country to provide education for all, would he be true to his word if by chance some millionaire family like Mitsui or Kōnoike[‡] adopted him? There is no end to fancies of this sort.

[†] [Fukuzawa borrows this passage from Franklin's *The Poor Richard's Almanack*. He also translated several passages from Franklin's works in his *Dōmō oshie gusa* (Teaching for School Children, 1872).]

[‡] [Fukuzawa is referring to the powerful merchant family, the Mitsui, which later became one of the financial conglomerates called zaibatsu. The Kōnoike was also a powerful merchant family which, unlike the Mitsui, gradually waned in the Meiji Period.]

They are all dreams caused by the fact that people do not compare the difficulty of a project with the duration of time it will take, and so are too generous and yet too superficial in their calculations.

Again, as I listen to those who undertake some business venture, I find that the majority say that they will accomplish it in, say, ten years time or within their lifetime. A small number reckon in one or three years, and hardly any say within a month, or right away. But I have never seen anyone who has already completed a project begun ten years ago. When people speak of something in the far-off future, they seem to be planning some great exploit, but when the scheduled date of completion finally draws near, they cannot clearly explain what the original project was. And this trouble is due, after all, to the fact that in the planning stage there was insufficient consideration of the time it would take to complete.

As I said above in reference to human affairs, men do more evil and more foolish things than they think. And they do not accomplish as much as they plan to accomplish. There are several ways to prevent this problem, but here is one which people seldom take notice of. And then what is it? It is occasionally to weigh in one's mind the success and failure, the gains and losses of an undertaking. To use a business analogy, it is a matter of taking stock and settling up accounts.

No one plans a business venture which will fail from the start. A man first thinks of his ability and capital, and looks over the business conditions of the world before beginning the undertaking. The business then sometimes succeeds and sometimes fails, depending on changing economic conditions. He may fail to stock some articles, or succeed in some sale. When he settles accounts at the end of a month or a year, sometimes things have gone as hoped, and sometimes not. Or when pressed with business he thinks that a certain article will sell well, but it sometimes turns out, contrary to his expectations, to be a loss on the balance sheet. Sometimes he thinks he is understocking himself. The reverse is true when it takes him more time than he expected to work off the unsold goods by the inventory day. Therefore it is most important in business to try to be timely in calculating sales potential, and to make a precise balance of accounts every day.

The same principle applies to other human affairs. Since the active business of human life begins from about one's tenth year when a person attains to the use of reason, people should endeavor daily to make a precise balance of accounts in the activities of business and in the attainment of knowledge and virtue, so as not to suffer losses in either. When a person examines his account books, he will always find some troublesome areas in regard to past or present actions. He should inquire: What have been the losses and gains in the past ten years? What business are you now engaged in, and how is it going? What articles are you now buying in, and when and where are they to be sold? Have you carefully supervised your store, or have you suffered losses because of the dissipation and laziness of your employees? Do you have sure prospects for the coming year? Are there other ways to increase your knowledge and virtue? Let me give one or two examples of these below.

The samurai who used to say that poverty was the usual lot of the samurai and the most important things were loyalty and patriotism, while they indiscriminately ate up the peasants' rice with haughty mien—but who today are in reality hard up—were like people who stocked swords, not knowing that there were foreign-made rifles. They made temporary profits, and then took great losses. Similarly, those who strongly believe in ancient things, who study only the old books of China and Japan to the exclusion of the ever-advancing Western Learning, are like persons who stock mosquito nets with the coming of winter, still mindful of the good business they enjoyed in the summer past. And young students who suddenly enter government service before their learning has matured, and therefore wander through the lowest-grade posts all their careers, are like those who pawn their half-made clothes and forfeit them. A person ignorant of the first steps in geography and history, who finds it difficult even to write everyday letters, but tries to plunge into works of high sophistication only to turn to another book after reading the first few pages, also resembles one who begins a business without capital and changes that business every day.

To continue this metaphor, a person who reads Japanese, Chinese, and Western books but does not know the world and national situation and can hardly manage himself and his family is like one who runs a general store without an abacus. A person who knows how to rule the country but not how to cultivate himself is comparable to one who advises his neighbors how to balance their accounts while his own house is being robbed. A man who likes to talk about the fashionable modern world but has no thoughts of his own in his head, even about himself, is like a person who knows the names but not the prices of goods. These faults are not uncommon in present-day Japan. They are caused by people drifting through life, never paying attention to their own situations and never examining their deeds from birth up to the present, or what they are doing now or should be in the future. Therefore I say that the final settlement of the account books is what clarifies business conditions and decides future prospects. In like manner, careful attention to his balance of knowledge and virtue as well as in business is what will clarify a person's present and future course.

THE MEANING OF THE WORD *SEWA*†

The term *sewa* has two meanings: (i) "protection" and (ii) "direct." The former means to stand by the side and watch over a person, or give him money or things, or spend time with him so that he will not lose profits or honor. The latter is something done for the good of a person. It means to give instructions concerning what is good and to protest against what is bad for another. It means to give advice to some one to the best of one's ability.

"Care" of others will be really meaningful and conducive to social order if it is done with both of the above meanings in mind. For example, if parents will take care of their children by providing for their everyday needs, children will obey their counsels and their home life will be tranquil. If the government makes good laws and takes good care of the people's lives, honor, and private property, and "protects" them by maintaining public order, the people will obey the government. Thus if nothing goes against this "counsel," the government and the people will be in harmony.

Therefore, "protection" and "counsel" have an area common to

---

† [The Japanese word that Fukuzawa uses is *Sewa* 世話 which means "care" in its commonest sense.]

both in which they are coextensive, with not even the slightest difference between them: where "protection" is provided, counsel should also be offered; where "counsel" is given, protection should necessarily be extended. But when they work at cross-purposes with each another, immediately trouble brews resulting in misfortune. There are not a few examples of this in society; they occur because people misinterpret the meaning of the word *sewa*. They sometimes interpret it to mean "protection" and sometimes to mean "counsel," but always one-sidedly, and this can lead to serious mistakes.

For example, if parents do not refrain from giving their dissolute son more money, and thereby foster his dissolute life, they may be giving him protective but not counseling care. And even if a child studies hard and obeys his parents' orders, for them to have him enter the harsh, uneducated and illiterate world without giving him enough food and clothing, means the parents have conversely only counseled him but been lax in protecting him. The former is an example of lack of filial piety, the latter of compassion. Both should be called evil human deeds.

There is an old saying about wearing out a welcome mat by calling on a friend too often. This means that excessive concern to advise someone who does not want it, or imprudent protesting to that person without knowing his temperament, will on the contrary result in that person hating, or resenting, or ridiculing us. As there is no benefit in this, the saying tells us to be careful not to bother him. This also means that where counsel does not apply, neither does protection.

Again, an elderly country gent in favor of the "good old days" may take out the genealogy of his main-family line and proceed to stir up trouble for a branch family. Or an uncle without money may summon his niece and give instruction to her about managing her own household, or may reproach her heartlessness and carelessness. Or even worse, he may try to take away her family's property, saying that it was in her grandfather's secret will. This would be a case of excessive counsel, without the slightest regard for protection. It is what a proverb calls unsolicited meddling.

Take also the instance of what is called relief for the poor, which looks only to the outward appearance of poverty and gives rice and money to the poor, regardless of whether they are good or not, and without inquiring about the causes of their poverty. It is reasonable to relieve those who are alone in the world without anyone to rely upon. But there are others who convert over half of their relief rice into sake. If they are indiscriminately given rice without anyone being able to counsel them to give up sake, it means that the protection far exceeds the counsel. Another proverb calls this "excessive sympathy." It is said that England has the same trouble with her own relief laws.

Broadening this principle and applying it to the national level, we find that people pay taxes and supply the needs of the government, thus supporting the household aspects of the government; but a despotic government disregards the suggestions of the people and blocks avenues of expression. Here protection has been accepted, but counsel has been blocked. From the point of view of the people, we can say that the government is also giving unsolicited protection.

It would be impossible to enumerate all the examples of this. Since the meaning of the word *sewa* is a most important part of economic theory, people of every walk of life should pay attention to it in their daily lives. The principle may seem to be entirely calculating and cold. But if a person tries to be sympathetic when he ought to be dispassionate, or colors the facts to make them seem more emotional than they are, and thereby ignores sincere feelings and makes human association unpleasant, it would be to give precedence to name over substance.

I have stated my main position above, but since I fear people's misunderstanding I will add a few more words here by way of further clarification. Some moral teachings seem to go contrary to economic laws. But in fact private virtue by no means affects the national economy. Sometimes a person will give money to a beggar who is a total stranger, without asking any questions. This may be a form of protection, but it is not given together with counsel.

If we discuss this problem [giving money to a beggar without counseling] by narrowing it down to the sphere of public economics, this act may seem to be improper, but the idea of giving a charitable donation should be most highly esteemed as a private virtue. For example, it is reasonable to have a law prohibiting beggars, but we should not reproach individuals who show charity to beggars. Dispassionate calculation cannot decide everything. It is essential to distinguish the proper spheres in which dispassionate calculation is appropriate. Scholars who are intoxicated with rational economic arguments should not forget that there is also room for the private virtues of love and kindness.

Section
FIFTEEN

METHODIC DOUBT AND SELECTIVE JUDGMENT

There is much that is false in the realm of belief, and much that is true in the realm of doubt. We need only consider how stupid people believe in other people's words, books, novels, rumors, the gods and Buddha, and fortunetellers. On the advice of a masseur they use grasses and herbs to cure a parent's mortal illness. At the time of the marriage negotiations over their daughter, they believe a fortune teller's analysis of the "physiognomy" of a suitor's house, and thus lose a good husband. Their faith in Amida prompts them to intone the *nenbutsu* instead of calling a doctor when they have a high fever. Because of their faith in Fudō Myō-ō they die after a twenty-one-day fast. In these cases, the quantity of truth is small indeed. But where truth is sparse, falsity cannot help being proportionately great. For even though these people believe in something or other, they are believing in false facts. Hence I say that there is much that is false in the realm of belief.

The progress of civilization lies in seeking the true facts both in the physical and the spiritual affairs of mankind. The reason for the West's present high level of civilization is that in every instance they proceeded from some irritation of doubt. Galileo [1564–1642] discovered that the earth is a planet by doubting the old theories of astronomy. Galvani [1737–98] discovered electricity in animals when he doubted the causes of convulsions in frogs' legs. Newton [1642–1727] discovered the principle of gravity when he saw an apple falling from a tree. Watt entertained doubts concerning the properties of steam when he was experimenting with a boiling kettle. In all these cases, they attained to the truth by following the road of doubt.

Leaving behind the investigations for natural laws, let me now turn to human progress. It was Thomas Clarkson [1760–1846] who put an end to a source of great social misery for later generations by calling into question the justice of the law of buying slaves. It was Martin Luther [1483–1546] who reformed the Christian faith through doubting the false teachings of the Roman religion. The French began the French Revolution by calling into question the authority of the *ancien régime*. The American colonists achieved their independence by calling into question the laws set up over them by England.

Even today the reason that the great persons of the West lead people along the path to higher civilization with ever-advancing theories is that their purpose is entirely to refute the once firm and irrefutable theories of the ancients, and to entertain doubts concerning practices about which common sense had never doubted before. For example, although it seems to be an almost natural human division of labor that the man should work outside the house and the woman keep order within it, John Stuart Mill [1806–73] wrote a book on women which attempted to destroy this custom which had been fixed and immovable since time immemorial. Many English economists advocated the doctrine of laissez faire, and its adherents believe it to be a universal law of economics. But American scholars proposed protective tariff laws. In fact, each country proposes its own economic theory. For every theory gives rise to a counter-theory, and disputes between rival theories never cease. In contrast to this ferment of ideas, the peoples of Asia have uncritically believed in foolish teachings, have been credulous of the gods and Buddhas, or have listened to the sayings of the so-called sages. They have not come under their influence only temporarily; they have been unable to escape from these ideas after thousands of generations. The quality of their deeds, the depths of their courage of mind and will, are incomparably less than the peoples of the West.

Pursuit of the truth when there is a conflict of different opinions is like sailing a boat against the wind. The boat's course must tack to the right and to the left. The high waves and strong winds may force it to sail through several hundred *ri* of water, while its straight-line course would come to no more than three to five *ri*. It is also possible to sail with a following breeze, but this is never so in human affairs. The course to the truth lies only by a zigzag course through the disputations of rival theories. And these theories all arise from doubt. Hence I have said that there is much truth in the realm of doubt.

Yet if it is true that we should not lightly believe things, we should also not uncritically doubt things, either. We must have insight into when to believe and when to remain skeptical. The essence of learning lies in clarifying this kind of discernment. Even in Japan, the sudden change in men's minds since the opening of our ports, the reforms in government, the overthrow of the nobility, the development of the school system, opening of newspapers, the new railroads, telegraph, military conscription, industries, etc.—the reform of a hundred old practices in a very short period of time—can all be said to have been the accomplishment of those who endeavored to effect these changes after calling into doubt customs which had been observed since time immemorial.

But still, such ancient customs have been called into question only since Japan has been opened to intercourse with the West. The reformers saw the superiority of Western civilization, and tried to imitate it. Therefore they were not motivated by self-originated doubt; they only believed in the new through the same faith with which they once believed in the old. The focus of men's minds that used to prevail in the East has only been redirected toward the modern West, but we have no guarantee that a truly critical choice has been made concerning present beliefs and doubts. I regret, of course, that due to my as yet shallow learning and limited experience I cannot enumerate in each and every case the rightness or wrongness of what is being accepted and discarded. But surveying the general trend of the changes in human life, it can be clearly shown that human mindedness tends to ride along with the times. Those who believe and doubt each go to extremes; neither side knows how far to go in believing or questioning the old or the new. Let me discuss the point further below.

East and West have had different customs, and especially different sentiments, for thousands of years. Even when their relative merits and demerits are clear, ancient customs cannot suddenly be interchanged from one country to another. This is all the more true in things whose merits and demerits are not yet clearly known. Our judgment as to the acceptance or rejection of these customs can only be made after their nature has been clarified through countless considerations over the course of years. But nowadays the somewhat better educated people of the middle class and above—those who are called "teachers of enlightenment"—are constantly declaiming the excellence of Western civilization. When one of them holds forth, ten thousand others nod their heads in approval. From teachings about knowledge and morality down to government, economics, and the minute details of daily life, there are none who do not applaud emulation of the ways of the West. Even those as yet barely informed about the West seem to be entirely abandoning the old in favor of the new. How superficial they are in uncritically believing and doubting things!

Now, the superiority of Western over Japanese civilization is certainly very great, but Western civilization is hardly perfect. I could never begin to enumerate all its defects. Its ways and customs are not all beautiful and credible; our customs are not all ugly and open to question. Let us consider the analogy of a young man who becomes a great admirer of his teacher. Wanting to emulate his teacher's manners, he quickly reforms his own mind, buys books and writing materials, and works hard day and night at his desk. This is, of course, commendable. But if he excessively imitates his teacher's ways, even the latter's bad habit of talking late into the night and rising late in the morning, thus ruining his own health in the bargain, shall we still call him intelligent? This youth regards his teacher as the complete scholar; regardless of his good and bad points, he imitates them all, and thereby brings himself to grief. There is an ancient Chinese proverb about imitating the eyebrows of Sei-shi.† The knitted brows of Sei-shi were attractive in themselves; therefore, it may still not be blameworthy to

---

† [A beautiful lady, Sei-shi of Yüeh, being sick, knitted her eyebrows. Since she still looked so beautiful, ugly women thought that if they did likewise they would become beautiful too. To the contrary, they only turned people off.]

imitate her. But what good can there be in the old scholar's late rising? Late rising is what it is, the vice of laziness and the neglect of health. To imitate another even to the point of his vices is surely the height of folly. Yet not a few of the proponents of enlightenment nowadays are like this young scholar.

Let us further probe, on the hypothesis that the customs and practices of East and West were reversed, what comment these teachers of enlightenment would give to each of the following cases. Imagine that Westerners bathed every day, while the Japanese barely once or twice a month; the teachers of enlightenment would exclaim that the people who are civilized and enlightened are always clean, stimulate their skin, maintain the laws of hygiene, etc., but the uncivilized Japanese do not understand these principles! If the Japanese kept a small chamber pot in their bedrooms at night, or did not wash after going to the bathroom, while the Westerners rose even in the middle of the night to go to the toilet and each time washed their hands, the proponents of enlightenment would declare that the enlightened Westerners place a high value on cleanliness, while the unenlightened Japanese do not know the meaning of the word, that they are like infants who are still too immature to distinguish cleanliness from filth! They would declare that the Japanese must imitate the beautiful customs of the West by advancing to the level of modern Western civilization. Or suppose that it was the Westerners who had the practice of using disposable paper handkerchiefs, while the Japanese used cloth ones which they used again after washing them. The proponents of enlightenment would exercise their wits and contrive clever sophistries about the great principles of economics, saying that in a country whose capital is low, the people naturally and unconsciously follow the principle of frugality. They would say that if the Japanese imitated the Western practice of using paper handkerchiefs to blow their noses, it would be wasting the country's resources. Therefore they endure this uncleanliness of using cloth handkerchiefs to be frugal, since they are pressed for lack of capital. Or if Japanese women hung gold rings from their ears, wore girdles, and pinned jewels on their dresses, the proponents of enlightenment would cite a bit of biological theory and raise serious objections about the terrible unenlightenment of the Japanese. They would say that not only do Japanese women not discern principles and follow nature, they are even damaging their health by hanging luggage from their ears. They would say that Japanese women are torturing their waists, which is the most important part of a woman's body, by making it like the waist of a wasp. They would further say that this prevents the chance of pregnancy and increases the dangers of childbirth, the calamity of which would bring sorrow to a family on a small scale, and damage the breeding of the nation's population on a large scale. And although Westerners barely use locks within and without the house, and although when they go on trips they hire porters to carry their luggage, which, while never locked, is never robbed, or although they order carpenters and plasterers to repair their homes without need of detailed contracts, but rarely go to court concerning breach of contract on a later day—if the Japanese on the other hand locked every room within the house, and put locks even on small chests by their side, and if they disputed and recorded every word on a contract, and yet things were still robbed and there were many cases of broken contracts brought to trial—the proponents of enlightenment would again sigh, saying how wonderful the holy teaching of Jesus Christ, and how pitiable the **pagans** outside of the Christian faith! It would look as if we Japanese lived in a den of thieves! Certainly, Japan cannot hold a candle in comparison with the customs of freedom and honesty in the West! Indeed, the countries in which the Holy Bible is preached would be exactly like the proverb says: so honest that people do not even pick things up off the roads. If the Japanese rolled and smoked cigarettes, while the Westerners used long pipes, they would declare that the Japanese lacked skill in making instruments and that was why they had not yet invented such pipes. If the Japanese wore shoes and Westerners wore *geta*, they would say that the Japanese did not know how to use their toes in wearing *geta*. If *miso* soup was brought on foreign vessels, it would not be thought of so lightly, as it is now. If *tōfu* [bean curd] was also found on the **tables** of the Westerners, its reputation would increase tenfold. Such dishes as baked eel or *chawan-mushi* [thick custard-like soup made with egg] would be praised as among the world's superlative dishes. I could enumerate these things endlessly. But let me go on to the more elegant matter of religious teachings.

If four hundred years ago a Saint Shinran was born in the West and a Martin Luther in Japan, and if Shinran had reformed the Buddhism practiced in the West and spread the Pure Land Buddhism teaching, while Luther had opposed the Roman religion of Japan and founded **Protestantism**, the proponents of enlightenment would certainly make the following evaluation. They would say that the great purpose of religion lies, not in killing, but in the salvation of all sentient beings: if this purpose is misconceived to any degree, the rest of its teachings are not worthy of consideration. In the West, Shinran embodied this principle. He slept in the fields with a stone for his pillow. At great cost and suffering he devoted the labors of his lifetime to reform his country's religion, so that today it is the religious faith of the majority of the people of the nation—so wide has his evangelism reached. And after Shinran's death, the fact that his disciples neither murdered men of other faiths nor were murdered for religious reasons can be said to have been entirely due to the merit of his teaching. But reflect, they would say, on how Luther came forward to challenge the old teachings of Rome. The Catholics did not easily succumb to his attack. The old and new teachings fought each other like a tiger and wolf, tooth and nail. After Luther's death, there occurred so many killings of Japanese citizens and so much waste of the nation's resources because of religious wars destructive of the nation, that they can neither be recorded with the pen nor spoken in words. The barbarous Japanese given to such slaughter visited such great sufferings on the souls of men because of the teachings of "universal salvation" and of "love thy enemy." As for the fruits of their accomplishments, Luther's Protestantism cannot be said to have been able yet to convert half of the people of Japan. Such are the differences of the religions of East and West, as would be told by the proponents of enlightenment!

I myself have entertained doubts about these things for a long time. But I still am not sure I have grasped the real causes of the great differences between the religions of East and West. When I ponder the matter privately, the following kind of questions come to my mind. Although Christianity preached in Japan and Buddhism in the West are similar in nature, is it that when practiced in a barbarous land they promote the spirit of killing, but create a spirit of tolerance in an enlightened country? Or do they differ in essence from the start? Or did Luther, the founder of the Japanese Reformation, and Shinran of the West differ greatly in the attainments of their virtue? The proponents of the enlightenment would say that these questions are not to be recklessly and superficially decided, but they defer them to the judgment of the scholars of future generations.

In terms of the above, our present-day reformers, who dislike the old customs of Japan and believe in the things of the West, cannot be said to have entirely escaped the criticism of having their own superficial beliefs and doubts. They believe in the new with the same blind faith with which they once believed in the old. In their excessive admiration of Western civilization, they emulate the vices of the West as well, like the women who imitated the knitted eyebrows of Sei-shi, or the student who imitated his master's late rising. Even worse, they reject the old even before they have been able to discover the new to believe in. Their persons are empty, as it were, having lost the qualities of spiritual peace and firm resolve. There have even been cases of insanity because of this. What a pity! (According to doctors' reports, incidents of nervous illness or insanity are on the rise in recent times.)

The civilization of the West is of course to be admired. But it is only recently that we have begun to do so; it would be better not to believe at all than to do so superficially. The West's wealth and power must truly be envied, but we must not go so far as to imitate the unequal distribution of wealth among her peoples as well. The taxes of Japan are not light, but if we consider the suffering of the poor people of England because of oppression by the landlord class, we should rather celebrate the happy condition of Japan's farmers. The custom of honoring women in the West is among the finest in the world, but if a wicked wife dominates and plagues her husband, or a disobedient daughter scorns her parents and gives free rein to disgraceful conduct, let us not be intoxicated over those customs.

Therefore, we can ask: Are the things being practiced in present-day Japan achieving their purposes as they are? Are Japanese business methods good as they now stand? Are the forms of government effective as they are now administered? Is the present system of education good as it is? Is the quality of books published now good as it is? Furthermore, are my present methods of research, following the modern way, good as they are? As I ponder these questions, a hundred doubts well up in me. It is as if I were now groping for something in the dark. Living in the very midst of these complex and intertwining problems, is it not difficult to compare things Eastern and Western, to believe and to doubt what should be and accept and reject what should be, with proper discernment? The responsibility of doing so falls today on no others than scholars such as ourselves. We must make every effort. To consider these problems there is nothing better than to study them. If, in pursuit of the truth, we read many books, touch upon many of these questions, and take a keen interest in them without anxiety or prejudice, we shall in due course be able to distinguish the areas of belief and doubt with clarity. Yesterday's beliefs may become tomorrow's doubts, and today's doubts may melt away in tomorrow's sun. Let us, therefore, make every effort as scholars.

Section
SIXTEEN

THE SPIRIT OF INDEPENDENCE IN EVERYDAY AFFAIRS

People talk these days about "freedom and independence" (*fuki dokuritsu*), but since there is apt to be much misunderstanding about what this really means, each of us should mark the point. There are two forms of independence, material and spiritual. Simply stated, one refers to things and the other to the mind.

The former means that each person in society may possess his own property and conduct his own business affairs, thereby providing for himself and his family without being a burden to others. In a word, it means not being dependent on others. Such material independence is something tangible; spiritual independence of mind has a profounder meaning and wider implications. It sometimes involves matters which appear to be unrelated to it, and so people are apt to misunderstand its meaning. Let me give an example, even though it is a trivial one.

A proverb says: "A man drinks the first cup of sake, but the third cup drinks the man." This means that desire for sake can end up controlling a man's mind, thus taking away his independence of mind. Nowadays, not only sake but any number of things can hinder the independent judgment of a person's mind. A man's *haori* coat does not match his clothes, and so he feels compelled to have another *haori* coat made. Or someone's tobacco pouch does not match his clothes, so he buys a second. Or if his clothes are well provided, his small house cramps his style of living. But when his new house is just finished, he feels constrained to celebrate with an extravagant dinner party. The dishes of rice and eel will further lead him to more extravagant Western dishes. Next he must buy a gold watch, and from this he progresses on to the next form of conspicuous consumption, and on and on endlessly. Considering these compulsions, we can compare him with a house without a master, a body without a mind. Things make people desire things. So the master has become the slave of his own desires.

I can give worse examples than these. In the former instance the persons were only slaves controlled by their own material desires. In other words, they were slaves only within the sphere of their own households. But consider the case of a person controlled by other people's possessions. Such is the person who is always aping someone else's tastes. He must have a new suit of Western clothes made because his neighbor has one. He must build a three-story house because his neighbor has built a two-story one. His friends' possessions become models for his purchases; his friends' conversations turn into a plan for his own order sheet. Or even though he knows full well that it is somewhat unbecoming for him, a tall and dark person, to wear a gold ring on his strong-jointed finger, he still feels compelled to come up with the money for one, thinking it is the Western custom. Or knowing quite well that it is best to wear a *yukata* and fan himself after a bath in the hot summer, he suffers under tight-sleeved Western shirts and suits, sitting there in his own sweat. His sole concern is to ape someone else's tastes.

As for his aping other person's likings, let's pass that over. But the most laughable kind of person is the one who misconceives what others actually have. Take, for example, the housewife who turns green with envy over the fact that her neighbor has bought a silk crepe and an ornamental hairpin of pure gold. She too has to order the same things. But later on she finds out that her neighbor's dress was made of cotton crepe and the hairpin was only gold plated. In all these cases, the compulsion came not so much from one's own possessions or those of others, but from one's own anxieties and delusions, which take complete control of the person's household. This frame of mind is far indeed from true independence of mind. Each person should take the measure of himself or herself.

A person's annual income of a thousand yen or his monthly salary of a hundred yen will all go down the drain as he exerts himself to live in this kind of dream world. As he unfortunately ruins his family fortune and annual or monthly income, the person then becomes despondent, and all he will have to show for it are useless household furnishings and a habit of luxury. What folly, beyond pity! He may expend his energies to build up wealth as the basis of personal independence, but only to lose that independence altogether as he falls victim to his own fortune. This is to lose independence by the same means used to seek independence. I am not praising the attitude of a skinflint, but I do hope that people would use their money in such a way that they, and not their money, are the masters of their minds.

THE COMPATIBILITY OF INTENTION AND ACTIVITY

People usually say that arguments should become deeds, but few ever get beyond the stage of just talking. Now, an argument is in a sense a written or verbal expression of one's views. When as yet unuttered or written down, it is called a person's motive or intention. It may be said that such an argument has nothing to do with things outside of oneself. In short, it is something within, something free and undetermined. Actual deeds express one's views outwardly, and, in contact with external things, engage them. Therefore deeds must necessarily be limited and, given the effect of external conditions, cannot be unbounded. In the past, people distinguished the ideas of "word and deeds," or "intentions and accomplishments." What is popularly called "views and actions" refers to the same things.

A "discrepancy between words and deeds" means that what one argues for and what one actually does do not tally. "To receive remuneration for work actually done and not for good intentions" means that you get paid for what you actually perform. Mere intentions are insubstantial, and not worthy of particular praise. Thus people sometimes say that a person may have various ideas, but he is essentially a good-for-nothing. This is another way of blaming the discrepancy between his claims and his actual deeds. Therefore claims and deeds must properly balance and coincide. For the convenience of my young readers I shall use the words *thought* and *work*, and try to make the point that when they do balance mankind can be benefited, and when they do not the opposite will be true.

First, there are different kinds of human works, of relative importance and magnitude. Acting in a dramatic play, doing scholarship, pulling a rickshaw, piloting a steamboat, farming with a hoe, writing books—these are all equally employments of man. But some men prefer not to become actors, and become scholars instead; or learn navigation rather than becoming rickshaw drivers; or prefer writing books to farming. Such people have passed over the relatively simpler tasks for more important jobs. We should praise such an attitude as the merit of a human being. What is it that has made them so discerning? It is their own minds, their own intentions, which were more refined and elevated. Therefore I am saying that men's minds must be elevated, and if not, their work cannot be so as well.

Secondly, some persons' works are of great and others of little use, regardless of their relative difficulty. Studying and making use of the arts of *go* and *shōgi* are no less difficult than studying astronomy, geography, mechanics, and mathematics. But they are far less useful. Those who can discern the relative usefulness of things and take the useful side are people of true original insight. If your mind is not insightful, you will exert yourself to no purpose.

Thirdly, there must be principles in a person's activities. There is a right time and place for our actions. For example, a sermon on morals is desirable, but if one starts to preach suddenly in the midst of merrymaking, he will only be laughed at. The stormy discussions of students are sometimes not uninteresting, but if they take place in a family gathering of women and children, it will be sheer insanity. The mind of a person who can discern the right time and place for them has clear insight. A person who acts without insight is like steam without an engine, or a boat without a rudder. Not only will he accomplish nothing, he will often do positive harm.

Fourthly, the above are examples of harms in which men have practical abilities but are careless in thought. There is also the contrary case where their thoughts are lofty, but they have no practical ability.

This too is quite out of balance. A person whose lofty ideas run out ahead of his actual abilities will be frustrated. He does not like to do work of which he is capable because it does not measure up to his ideals. But he is too deficient in practical ability to give his mind full play, and so he does not do anything at all. Thereupon, instead of blaming himself, he reproaches others, or says his proper opportunity never came or he had no luck. It seems as if he is possessed by the idea that there was no work for him to do anywhere. Consequently he withdraws to brood by himself. He complains with a querulous face that others are his enemies and unkind to him. His attitude is like that of one who reproaches someone else for not promptly returning money that was in fact never lent.

All the livelong day there seems to be only grief and unhappiness. The Confucian scholars grieve that no one understands them. Students deplore the fact that there is no one to give them correct guidance. Government officials complain that they cannot find the secret to rising up the ladder of success. Merchants grumble over bad business conditions. After the abolition of the *han* (domain), the ex-samurai deplored the fact that they could not make a living; peers out of office complained of lack of respect.

Everyone is grumbling these days. As proof of this, just watch people's sour faces in their daily intercourse with each other. How few there are whose speech and looks are cheerful and full of life! In my own experience, I am always meeting gloomy and never cheerful ones. Many could lend their faces to condolence cards. What a pity! If each person could just be made to work according to his ability, he would naturally relish his work, and gradually grow his business. Then he would finally come to harmonize his aspirations and actual deeds. But people never think like this. Their aspirations run way ahead of their deeds, and as they want more and more but attain nothing, they are endlessly frustrated. They are like a stone image of *Jizō* infused with the soul of a postal courier, or like a paralyzed patient whose nerves have become extremely sensitive. From this we may judge how great people's grievances and frustrations are.

Again, a person with noble mind but poor practical ability is sometimes disliked and isolated by others. His work is, of course, inferior to others. But from his own point of view he finds faults only in others. Naturally and privately he regards others with contempt. It is without question that people who despise others more than necessary cannot avoid being despised in turn. They will finally ridicule each other as being eccentric and queer, and will not associate with each other. In my view, some people are disliked by others because of their own arrogance and insolence, or because they desire to get the better of others, or are too demanding, or slander others. They fail always to make a true comparison of themselves with others. They make their own noble intentions the criteria with which to judge others. They then create enchanting fancies about themselves which only arouse the hatred of others. Finally they withdraw from others' company and fall into despondency and loneliness.

Let me therefore say to the younger generation: if you are dissatisfied with another person's efforts, go and do it yourself. If you think another's business is poorly done, just try to do better. Put your own household in order if you think your neighbor's household is not. Write a book yourself before commenting on another's. Before you comment on a scholar or a doctor, become one yourself. If you want to meddle in another's work, no matter how trivial, put yourself in the other's shoes and then examine yourself. Or if someone else's job is completely different from yours, make a fair estimation of the relative difficulty and importance of his work. Even if his work is different, you will not make a great mistake as long as you compare just the practical ability of yourself and the other person's.

Section
SECTION SEVENTEEN

ON POPULARITY

A person to whom many others look up and point as trustworthy and reliable may be called popular. He is one who inspires confidence in people in whatever calling he pursues and in whatever job he takes on, and for whom society has great expectations. The human world has people of various degrees of popularity; if a person cannot be accredited even in the slightest degree, he will be of no use at all. To take a small example, a person who is sent on an errand to buy something worth ten *sen* is trusted to that amount, and is accredited by others to that amount. Passing from ten *sen* to one yen, from one yen to a thousand, ten thousand, and finally to a person who manages a bank having a reserve of several million yen, or again to a governor of a prefecture or ministry, not only do they have charge over money, but also over the welfare, wealth, and honor of their fellow citizens. Therefore unless persons in such important tasks are looked up to by their fellow citizens and have their confidence, it will be very difficult for them to do their proper jobs. Not to trust them in such instances would be to call their integrity or ability into question. There will be no limit to distrusting them.

There are many examples, both past and present, of strange anecdotes told about how the anxieties of men were exasperated by placing *metsuke* [feudal censors] to spy on one other, or by ordering inspectors to inspect other inspectors, etc., but without ultimate success. There are also many people who buy without checking the quality of the products of Mitsui or Daimaru,† thinking that since their policy is to mark prices on price tags, there will be no overcharges. And there are many who think that the works of Bakin‡ must certainly be interesting, and so they order them just on account of the titles. Accordingly the stores of Mitsui and Daimaru and the works of Bakin become increasingly popular. Such popularity is a great convenience to business and the writing of books. Even from such examples we can know the importance of a good name.

Now the question of popularity or good name is beside the point when talking about putting a 16 *kan* [60 kg] weight on the back of a person who has the power to lift it, or about lending one thousand yen to a person who has an estate worth that amount. For these are entirely questions of whether the person can in actual fact handle the added weight or repay the debt. But the affairs of men are generally not as plain and simple as that. Even a person who cannot lift ten *kan* can sit down and move several hundred *kan*, or a person whose estate is not worth a thousand yen can put several tens of thousands of yen in circulation. If we suddenly broke into the accounting rooms of merchants who have the reputation of being financial barons and made a precise calculation of their books, there would be some that were short several hundred or several thousand yen in their accounts. Even though such shortages amounted to more than the property owned, so that these men were several hundred or thousand times worse off than a penniless beggar, society nonetheless would not compare them to beggars. Why is this? This is because the merchants have credit. Accordingly, public reputation does not essentially lie in having great competence or properties. It is something gradually acquired through an alert and clever mind, and by the virtue of an honest character.

That popularity is connected with knowledge and virtue is rational and inevitable, but still there have been not a few cases of its opposite in public affairs in both ancient and modern times. Phony doctors have

---

† [Daimaru was a dry-goods store founded in 1717, and still exists today as one of the biggest department store groups in Japan.]
‡ [Kyokutei (a.k.a. Takizawa) Bakin (1767–1848) was a popular author of a Japanese literary genre called *gesaku*. He completed his major romance, *Nansō Satomi hakkenden* (Eight Dog Chronicles), over a period of 28 years from 1814 to 1842. This work is regarded as one of the representative *yomihon* ("reading books"), a literary style established in the Edo Period, which placed greater emphasis on the contents of the text than on its illustrations.]

enlarged their office entrances and become prosperous. Apothecaries have put up gold signboards and widened their sales of medicines. Speculators have placed empty safes by their desks. Scholars have adorned their study rooms with original sources which they could not even read. People riding home in rickshaws read newspapers, only to feel drowsy and have to take a nap. The same people who weep tears in church on Sunday afternoon fight with their spouses on Monday morning. Throughout the nation, honest and false, good and bad, are intermingled. Which can be called which? Even worse, a few people, in view of their very popularity, worry whether they are ignorant or immoral. It is no wonder that somewhat high-minded gentlemen do not seek fame or deliberately avoid it as the vainglory of the fleeting world. This is one of the commendable points in the attitude of a gentleman.

Nevertheless, if we discuss only the extreme cases in the affairs of society, there is nothing without its potential harm. That a gentleman does not seek fame in the world seems to be praiseworthy, but he must first clarify the nature of fame before he decides to seek or not seek it. If his fame runs to the extreme of vainglory, like the doctor's entrance or the apothecary's signboard, it should of course be repudiated. But from another point of view, human affairs are not all motivated by vanity. The knowledge and virtue of men are like flowering trees; fame and popularity are their blossoms. When cultivating trees to bear flowers, there is no reason purposely to suppress their blooming. Not carefully understanding the nature of fame and trying to cast it away is like clearing off the blossoms and ending up losing its charms. There would be no particular merit in doing so. It would be no different from treating living things as dead. This would be very harmful to the public good.

Yet, should we *seek* fame and reputation? I say, yes, we should. But it is imperative that we do so according to our station and abilities. Winning popularity through mental and physical activities should be like measuring out rice to give to others. Those who are skilled at measuring out one *to* of rice with a *masu* may sometimes under-measure it to the extent that there will be as much as three *gō* left over;† and those who are not skillful

---

† [A *masu* is a unit for measurement. One *to* is about eighteen liters, and one *gō* is a hundredth of a *to*]

may over-measure it so that there will be a shortage of about the same amount. When I advocate seeking popularity according to one's station and abilities, I mean to measure the one *to* of rice exactly as one *to*, neither more nor less. While there is relative skill in measuring rice, the difference caused by it is only two or three per cent. But in the case of marking the measure of one's own talent and virtue, the tendency is to overestimate or underestimate oneself by far more than three per cent. The skillful person will inflate himself two or three times over, and the unskillful person will underestimate himself by as much as half his real worth. The excessive degree of the former will be a source of great harm to others, and of course is to be despised. But passing over that for a while, let me here say a few words concerning the person who underestimates himself.

Confucius teaches that the gentleman does not grieve over not being known by others, but grieves that he does not know others. This teaching was meant to correct abuses which were current in his own time. But spiritless and unprincipled Confucians of later times have taken these words at face value. By interpreting this as withdrawal from the world, their harm has gradually increased, and finally they have become eccentric, speechless, and emotionless men, like pieces of wood, which neither laugh nor cry. It is a curious fact that people look up to these men, and that they are even called elegant teachers. It is necessary to divest ourselves of these base customs and enter into the spheres of energetic life. That is, we must have broad experience in the world of things and men, both to be known and to know men, and to give full play to our inherent abilities. In order to be able to accomplish this for personal and social good, the following qualities are necessary.

(I) A person should study the art of speaking. To make one's ideas known through the written word is of course a powerful means, and naturally one should not neglect this path or give up his intention of writing correspondences and books. But there is no more effective means than direct speaking to get one's thought across to others at first hand. Therefore one must strive to be as eloquent and vigorous as possible in speech. In recent times, meetings featuring public speaking have been held, and it has of course been beneficial to hear useful discussions at those meetings. Both speakers and listeners have been able to share in the benefit to be obtained from fluent and eloquent discourses. But as I listen to the poor speakers of today, I find that their vocabulary is quite limited. They somehow seem to be at a loss for words and expressions.

Take, for example, the case of a schoolteacher lecturing on some translation. If the subject is that of "round crystal jewels," the teacher makes no explanation of what the phrase means, taking it for granted that the students already know it. He only glares at them, saying that it means a round crystal jewel. But if this teacher had a rich vocabulary and mastery of expression, he could say that "round" means something like a rice ball with its corners smoothed off, that "crystal" is something like glass mined from the mountains, much of which is produced in Kōshū, and that this crystal has been shaped into a jewel like a rolling ball. If he explained it in these terms, even women and children could perfectly understand him. That he has a hard time due to his not employing words that are pertinent, indicates he has not learned the art of public speech. Or take the case of some students who utter meaningless nonsense to the effect that they have to use English because Japanese is so inadequate that they can neither write nor make speeches properly in it. It seems to me that these students, though born in Japan, are still not proficient in their own mother tongue. Every national language increases in sophistication in proportion to the complexity of the country's affairs, and therefore people should not suffer any inconvenience in using it. More than anything else, present-day Japanese must strive for fluency and eloquence in their own language.

(II) It is necessary to have a cheerful demeanor, and not give a first impression which turns people off. To perk up one's shoulders and smile fawningly, to be a smooth talker, a drum-beater, or a flatterer, are of course detestable manners. But it is just as detestable to have a grumpy and gloomy face; to have the look of one praised for being taciturn but reproved for smiling; to have the look of one suffering from chest pains all his life; or to have a constant look of one in mourning for his dead parents. A cheerful and lively countenance is one mark of a man of true virtue; in social intercourse it is quite essential. A person's countenance is like the door to his home. To have a wide circle of friends and callers who feel welcome, he must first open his gate, scrub clean the entrance, and show pleasure in their arrival. But people nowadays go to the opposite extreme. They greet others with sour looks, in imitation of the pseudo-gentlemen, and are like people who put skeletons before their entrances and coffins before their gates. Who would want to call on them?

France is said to be the source of civilization and the center of knowledge in the world. The reason for this is, among other things, that the French people's activities are always lively and cheerful, and they have a spirit of warmth in their speech and appearance.

Now, it may be said that speech habits and appearance are inborn; it being impossible to change them, it is useless to argue about them. While this seems true, it turns out to be incorrect when we consider the natural law of human intelligence and its development. Generally speaking, the power of human intellect will advance as much as it is made to advance. It is exactly like strengthening one's muscles through physical exercise. Our habits of speech and appearance, which are also movements of the body and mind, cannot be improved through neglect. So has it not been a great mistake from ancient times that in Japan men have not cultivated these important functions and have not cared about them? I am not saying that the Japanese *must* make a study of speech and appearance, but I hope that from the present on they will at least *begin* to take proper notice of these efficacious ethical precepts.

Someone may still object that to make one's appearance presentable only means to adorn one's looks on the outside. And if such is made the essence of human association, people will not only adorn their looks and their clothes and foods, and the like, they will even invite guests whom they normally would not think of inviting and entertain them in a style inappropriate to their social standing. Thus, there will be vices in human association motivated by affectation.

Yes, such an objection also seems to contain some truth; but as we can see in the saying, "Too much is as bad as too little," affectation is an abuse, not the essence, of human association. Thus for example the purpose of food is to nourish the body, but overeating will injure one's health. Nutrition is the purpose of taking food, overeating its abuse— thus each is the opposite of the other. The aim of human association is also to be harmonious and sincere, whereas indulging in ostentatious role-playing is not the true essence of human relationships.

No relations are as intimate as those between husband and wife and between parents and children. What, then, governs such intimate relationships? It is a sincere heart that is harmonious and honest. Intimate relations can be realized only when affectation has been swept away. In like manner human friendship is based on sincerity, which is entirely incompatible with ostentation. I say this to show people the direction in which they should strive, even though I do not expect people to treat others with the same affection as they treat their spouses or parents or children. These days people rightfully praise a person for being cheerful, open-hearted, free and easy, frank, manly, talkative but moderate in pressing his views, boisterous but lovable, taciturn but kind, or serious looking but frank, and the like. These qualities are all family-like qualities, and put a premium on sincerity and harmony with others.

(III) Another saying has it: "If people walk different paths, they will never meet to discuss matters together." People also misunderstand this saying. Birds of the same feather tend to flock together—scholars with scholars, doctors with doctors, and so forth. If slightly diverging in their occupations, they do not remain close to one another. When they were schoolmates they were friends, but after graduation each goes his own way, becoming a merchant or a government official, etc., and drifting miles apart, even becoming enemies in some cases. What a tragic result!

If we wish to interact with others, we should not only remember our old friends but also make new ones. We should meet with one another in order to communicate with each other. If we do not, there is no way to know each other. Are there not many gentlemen who have met someone by chance and have become his friend for life? When we meet people, there is one chance in ten of making a real friend, and two chances in twenty. And it is mainly in such a way that we get to know one another. Therefore, over and above the question of popularity and fame, it is a good thing to have many acquaintances and friends. You may meet someone on the Ginza who was in the same ferryboat with you years back, and the two of you may now unexpectedly have something to offer each other. A greengrocer who delivers at your house may someday be there to take care of you when you fall ill at some inn along the highway to Ōshū.† Men are neither devils nor serpents. They are not

---

† [Fukuzawa is referring to Ōshū Dōchū (a.k.a. Ōshū kaidō; Oshu Highway), one of the Five Highways in the Edo Period. It connected Edo with present-day Shirakawa City and other parts of northern Japan.]

enemies out to harm you. Let us welcome people into our lives in a natural way, with true and open minds.

In addition, if we want to widen our circle of friends, it is essential to have as broad a range of interests as possible. We have to be able to play more than one note ourselves, and this means we should associate with people of all sorts of interests—intellectual interests, business interests, calligraphy and art, the games of *go* and *shōgi*. Except for dissipation, everything can become an avenue to friendship. People of no accomplishments whatever can still enjoy a meal or tea together. On an even lower level, people with strong builds may find they can acquire new friends in such games as arm wrestling, pillow tug-of-war and leg-wrestling.† It may seem that arm wrestling and intellectual activities do not belong in the same categories. But the world is large and human associations multifarious. Our lives should be different from that of a few crucian carp passing their days in the bottom of a well. People should not dislike one another.

---

† [In the game "pillow tug of war," two opponents take hold different ends of a Japanese wooden pillow, using only the tips of their fingers. Each strives to pull the pillow away from the other. In "leg-wrestling," two opponents are seated and strive to knock each other, using only their legs.]

APPENDIX TO

AN ENCOURAGEMENT OF LEARNING

Appendix

A DEFENSE OF *GAKUMON NO SUSUME*

By Gokurō Senban,† Keio-gijuku, 1874

THERE have been many recent attacks on Mr. Fukuzawa's *Gakumon no susume* (Encouragement of Learning). These attacks seem mostly to have been aimed at Sections Six and Seven. Intelligent people have the right to express their views, of course, and I am not venturing to refute these critics to cajole public opinion. But I find that there are many who seem to make rash criticisms of only a section or a phrase of the book, or without even closely examining Sections Six and Seven that are the main targets of these attacks. This motivates me to express my own view in public here.

Section Six of *Gakumon no susume* discusses the importance of the national constitution, and condemns the evil of private vendetta. It says that when people are subject to a government, they have completely entrusted the power over life and death to it, and so no longer have any right to that power. In application of this principle, Fukuzawa says that even in an extreme case when a burglar breaks into one's home, the

---

† Gokurō Senban 五九樓仙萬 was the pseudonym used by Fukuzawa in his vindication of Section Seven of An Encouragement of Learning against the charge that he had equated the loyalty of a male servant (of some household) named Gonsuke with the heroic Imperial loyalism of the fourteenth-century warrior, Kusunoki Masashige. It is illustrative of the well-known Nankō-Gonsuke controversy which An Encouragement of Learning set in motion in its day. This article appeared on 7 July, 1874 in Chōya shinbun (Chōya Times).

owner has no right recklessly to lay his hands on the man. After illustrating the evil of private vendetta in this way, he ends Section Six by discussing the cases of the loyal retainers of Akō and other assassinations of political enemies. This is my interpretation of Section Six.

As indicated at the beginning, Section Seven supplements the argument of Section Six. For the convenience of understanding, it divides the citizens' roles into that of masters and guests. In the latter role, once they have made the contract, thus promising to live as guests under the Meiji government, the citizens have no right to take inconveniences of the laws as a pretext to break the laws. This principle proclaims the rightful authority of the government. From the former role of the people as masters, in which capacity they support the government's expenses and entrust the public welfare to the government, the people must shoulder both the losses and gains of the government. If they disagree with the government's measures, they must quietly report and discuss their views without hesitation. The purpose of the principle is to make every citizen of Japan consider his country as his own home and to defend the independence of Japan.

In the middle paragraphs of Section Seven, Mr. Fukuzawa discusses the question of changing the government. He raises the difficult issue of what should be done if the government neglects its duty and becomes despotic. He gives three options of action. First, to compromise principles by yielding to the despotic government, thus leaving a bad precedent for later generations and weakening the country: he says that persons of true and patriotic hearts would not act in this insincere way. Secondly, to rise up against this despotic government with force of arms: here he argues that this course of action toward rebellion is incomparably worse and should never be done. Thirdly, to live under tyrannical government while adhering to one's principles even at the cost of **martyrdom**: the purpose of this positive idea is strictly to suppress violence in favor of persuasive reason. As this section was an abridged translation of page 366 of Wayland's *Morals*, let me translate the passage which comes right after the section Mr. Fukuzawa translated, by way of supplementing the reader's information.

We read on page 367:

In England during the reign of Charles I, people could no longer endure the tyranny of the government, and public criticism was aroused. Finally, after a civil war, the king was dethroned and a republican government was temporarily set up. But the people continued to be repressed under it too. This government came to an end several years later, and Charles II ascended the throne, but the government became increasingly despotic. It was as if the English had lost their freedom by seeking it, and bought tyranny with tyranny. This shows how wrong rebellion is. During Charles II's reign, the popular spirit changed. Instead of relying on violence, people advocated reason and continued to sacrifice their lives for the sake of principle. Through their **martyrdoms** they laid the foundation for the freedom and independence of modern England.

At the end of the section, Mr. Fukuzawa deals with the question of **martyrdom**. He compares it with rebellion, and discourses on the relative merits of each. He says that loyalty should be valued as a human act, but there is no reason to make it an end in itself and to think that loyalty is the mere giving of one's life for one's lord. As for his example of the faithful servant, Gonsuke, who hung himself, if we pass over the circumstances of his death to consider only his death itself, we cannot help calling it too a kind of dying out of the motive of loyalty. It was no different in that regard from the death of a loyal retainer. But, then, should Gonsuke's death not become a model for men? By no means, for his death was no more than a stubborn dog's death, since it gave no benefit to civilization.

As for the question of loyal samurai and loyal retainers of past history, we can see that there were many indeed who died for their country or their lord. When the Hōjō clan perished and Takatoki killed himself, six thousand eight hundred men committed suicide with him. Even though Takatoki was a rebel, we must say that those who followed him in suicide were loyal retainers of the Hōjō house. In addition to this case, innumerable retainers died for their lords on both sides when the Takeda and Uesugi clans clashed in battle. But from our present vantage point, for what reason did they give their lives? Mr. Fukuzawa points out that if the Takeda and Uesugi clashed in arms in modern Japan, we could not help saying that the samurai who died in battle were throwing away their lives in vain.

Moreover, we can make this same point by citing the examples of foreign countries. In the past, France and Spain fought religious wars. Countless numbers killed others or died in battle at the command of their rulers. The loyalty of these persons was no cause for shame, but seen through the eyes of modern European civilization, those who perished in these religious wars died like dogs.

Why do I say that the loyal retainers and faithful samurai died also like dogs as they followed their lord to the grave? In the uncivilized world of that time, men's purposes went no further than their own individual spheres of action. They did not extend their gaze to the peace and prosperity of the nation as a whole. This was not their own fault, but the forces of the times. In the past, their deaths were expressions of loyalty; but today, they would be meaningless and in vain. Therefore later times may admire their intentions, but should not ape their deeds.

Now in No. 368 of the *Chōya Times*, a certain gentleman of Aikodō criticizes Mr. Fukuzawa for arguing that the forty-seven samurai of Akō had no purpose to advance civilization and declares that his censure of them is difficult to understand. But if we consider the changes in history and civilization several hundred years since, there should be no objection to acknowledging that the people of olden times did not have the ideals of modern civilization. But this was no shame upon those men of old. We must highly prize the attainment of civilization in modern times, but this is not a reason to credit modern men at the expense of the ancients. The men of past history lived in their own times and acted according to their own values; modern people must now act according to modern values. In such a way each age fulfils its function of being human.

Kusunoki Masashige's name does not appear within the text of *Gakumon no susume*. But as society has interpreted Mr. Fukuzawa's intention in this manner, let me discuss that here. It is not necessary to speak at great length about the loyalty and courage of Masashige. The question is, did Mr. Fukuzawa mean to equate Masashige with the Gonsuke in his text? Did he say that if Gonsuke had fought as well as

Kusunoki Masashige in the Genkō and Shōhei Revolts, there would be no difference in their merits? I can attest that he never expressed such an idea either in writing or in his speech. The focus of Mr. Fukuzawa's essay was on the revolutions of the times, on history prior to and after the advent of modern civilization. The only point on which he compared Gonsuke with that loyal knight was that of their deaths. The loyal samurai Masashige was like a sword blade made by Masamune, Gonsuke like a rusty kitchen knife. Considered in terms of the dignity of their activities and merits, their deaths cannot be compared, even though, in the above metaphor, both the Masamune blade and kitchen knife may be made of iron. It would affront human reason even to entertain their comparison; indeed, it is ridiculous even to hear it said. If a person has any genuine human sentiment at all, he will distinguish the two cases. When Kusunoki established his merit in the Genkō and Shōhei Revolts, he flashed the aforementioned sword of quality. When he plotted for the sake of the Imperial House, his sword alone flashed in the land. Therefore the greatness of Masashige lay not in his death, but in his actions. And what did his actions purport? Their goal was to restore the political authority of the nation for the Imperial House. As deeds for those times, they are above all criticism. He fulfilled his duty to the utmost.

Yet if we consider the matter from the changes of history from the medieval world to the Meiji Period, the present goals for which the Japanese people must strive are greatly different. During the Genkō and Shōhei revolts, the usurpers of the political prestige of the Imperial House were the Hōjō and the Ashikaga. The seat of political power had shifted internally within Japan, but in terms of blood line, the emperors of the Northern Court were also Imperial princes. While there may have been rebellious ministers and subjects from ancient times, even Masashige did not anticipate that anyone would suddenly try to usurp the Imperial dignity. And Masashige was discontent with the situation that had ensued. To the very end, he gave his strength and his life fighting for the true line of succession, and to return its political authority to the Imperial House. In certain respects, these events were very regrettable. But it was not that the Imperial dignity had finally been usurped by foreign hands. Since it had not, Masashige may have had the hope of regaining it for the Emperor; although he was ultimately frustrated, he must have had this one ray of hope. Therefore, compared with the foreign threat which the present Japanese people have to cope with in the Meiji Period, Masashige's situation was far more sustainable. His burden was far lighter than the present responsibility of the Japanese people. This is a result of the changes of history from the pre-modern to the modern world. Let us not forget this essential point. The present crisis is in fact the first and the most serious one for Japan since the founding of the Japanese empire.

The prime source of grievance for Japan in the Meiji Period has been relations with the West. In commercial transactions, the Westerners are wealthy and skillful, we Japanese are poor and unskillful. In the jurisdiction of the courts, many Japanese citizens suffer injustices, while some of the foreigners escape the law. We have to learn foreign methods of study, and borrow their foreign capital. Since our policy is gradually to open the country and follow the direction of modern civilization, they assert the principle of free trade to gain sudden access to the interior of Japan. In every matter they take the offense and we the defense, with never a proper balance between us. As these conditions are accelerating, unless we Japanese amend our old customs, the prestige of Japan will inevitably decline, even if no war breaks out with the West. Indeed, in the event of some unforeseen crisis, it could decline even more. Considering this threat, we have just cause for genuine alarm.

In these difficult times, it is not enough to think that each Japanese citizen fulfils his obligation simply by saying that he is ready to offer his life in case of emergency. This is certainly not my opinion. The political authority of the Genkō and Shōhei times fell into the hands of Ashikaga Takauji, but there can be no Takauji in the Meiji Period. Our present formidable enemies are in reality the countries of the West. This was the meaning of Mr. Fukuzawa's allusion to "the bold and dauntless foreigners" in Section Three of *Gakumon no susume*. If Japan loses her sovereignty today, her political authority will not merely pass from the Imperial House but from the shores of Japan. If it passes from the Imperial House, there is still some hope of recovering it; but if it passes to foreign hands it will never be recovered. How can we follow the same path of India? We must focus our attention upon the relative values of things. Can we imitate the deeds of Masashige in these present times of crisis? I am saying that we cannot. We must admire his spirit, but not take his deeds as our model. As we see in the above example, Masashige's deeds were like a Masamune sword. In the age of swords, this Masamune sword was considered the finest of weapons. But with the changes of history, even this superlative weapon became useless, and it was necessary to devise other instruments. This is precisely the way of change.

There was no danger from foreign countries in the age of Masashige. Because there was none, there was no need to respond to it. It was not Masashige's fault that he acted as he did, for such were his times. But present-day scholars excessively admire his aspirations and loyalty, and think that his deeds should still be emulated. It seems that some persons are in fact trying to apply his ancient deeds unchanged to the needs of the present. To use a metaphor, this is no different from employing ancient-style spears and swords in an age of rifles. This is the reason why I doubt the efficacy of their ideas. As I view Masashige, if he were brought back to life today, I think he would take upon himself the responsibility of the independence of Japan. He would work for the rights of every Japanese citizen, for the general security and prosperity, for Japan's national strength, and thereby preserve the continuity of the Imperial House. He would work to make the national polity (*kokutai*) one and indivisible and to make it increasingly beam forth its light. He would strive to bring Japan up to a level of equality with all the nations of the world. For these are the great principles of civilization today. In order to accomplish these great tasks, how can we rely only on one death, like Masashige's of old? The present times call for adaptability in ten thousand new forms.

If Russian or English warships showed up today to invade the harbor of Hyōgo, Masashige would certainly not be satisfied with merely sacrificing his own life as he did at Minatogawa. I cannot venture to guess what his method of responding to the present crisis would be, but we can know that he would have changed his strategy. In the last analysis, death is a deed of the flesh; mediocre men can die in vain by killing themselves like dogs. Adaptability is a work of intelligence; it is the power to discern the relative values of things and the momentum of the times. Masashige was hardly a mediocre man. If alive today, he would certainly concentrate his view on the whole situation. Since today's crisis is different from the Genkō and Shōhei times, he would take another course of action and give his life in a different way. The ancient dispute was an internal one, but the Meiji crisis comes from abroad, and is much graver. This is the reason why Masashige's action in the Meiji Period would be different from the days of old.

Therefore, one who admires the personality of Masashige and would make him a model of the present age should imagine what course of action his hero would really take in our Meiji times and strive to follow that action as his rule. Only in this manner will we be able to say that he has understood the true spirit of Masashige. A man who thinks that the Masashige of medieval times would act in the same manner today, so many hundred years later, has not yet fully understood him. On the contrary, we may say that he really despises him, and this is something which we must regret for Masashige's sake. Even though Masashige's loyalty would perdure unchanged throughout all time, his actions would not be immutably the same. This is the precise reason why Masashige was the person that he was.

When I speak of adaptability, some high-spirited young people may rashly take this as a cowardly excuse. But let us think about it with composure. That Hōjō Tokimune beheaded the envoy from the Mongol Court during the Kōan Period may well be called a rightful deed. But what if Tokimune lived in the Meiji Period and beheaded an envoy from Russia or England; of if some Meiji citizen should imitate Tokimune's deed at the present time? It would be sheer madness. Why is it that the identical act of the killing of an envoy is regarded as justice in the old times and as madness today? For the times are different. We are at a different stage of civilization. Generally speaking, everything will be adaptable if its historical time and place are not disregarded. Such is the way of adaptability.

I take the above as the main import of Mr. Fukuzawa's argument. Considering the above points, we cannot say that he did not understand Masashige. We may rather say that he understood Masashige better than most informed people. The reason that *Gakumon no susume* has stimulated such a mass of bewildering debates of late is that both sides are clashing over unessential points without either side expressing its main view. In all probability the newspaper contributors have the most patriotic intentions, but they are not as keen as Mr. Fukuzawa in perceiving the problems connected with foreign relations. They are not so thoroughgoing in the pursuit of national independence, not so clear-sighted in discerning the changes of the times and in weighing the relative priorities of things. Thus they end up digressing into arguments over unessential points. I believe that Mr. Fukuzawa has no need to worry himself over these loud public criticisms. Rather, he must be concerned about the superficiality of the controversy in the context of modern problems.

Other attacks against Mr. Fukuzawa have come from those who want to refute his remarks about republican government, Christianity, etc. Here they are completely off the track! To say that Mr. Fukuzawa advocated republican government or was attracted to Christianity is wrong. From what document or from what person has this information been gotten? Mr. Fukuzawa advocates democracy because he dislikes the despotism prevalent in the world today. He states his views publicly, not privately.

Japan has also had from ancient times a deep-rooted tradition of despotic governments, because of which her spirit has declined and there is fear that the Japanese people cannot bear up under foreign relations. Accordingly Mr. Fukuzawa's original intention was to maintain Japanese independence by correcting this abuse as much as possible. His idea is to counter one-sided governmental authority by stressing the rights of the people, and thus to develop the power of the whole nation against the foreign threat. One must first distinguish matters under discussion, such as republican government, Christianity, people's rights, despotism, etc. Mr. Fukuzawa hates despotic tyranny. And on this he is not alone, for every human being hates it. There is no reason to say "only Fukuzawa, a crazy man, hates it." Again, religion and politics are entirely different things. As regards religion, too, he has expressed his views for many years. I need not repeat them here. (If people listened sympathetically to what he has to say on religion, they would surely be amazed at the profundity of his views.) Must despotism and tyranny necessarily accompany monarchy, and freedom and human rights only be realized under a democratic form of government? What books and whose utterances are the sources of such inferences? I should like to discuss this point a little further in closing.

Despotism is like a fever, and politics is the human body. Persons differ in sex and age, but they are all capable of contracting a fever. In politics, too, there are different kinds, such as a monarchy and a republic, but they may all become despotic. A despotic monarchy derives from one person's ideas, while misgovernment in a democracy stems from a number of people. But both are equally forms of despotism. They are like two human beings who are capable of coming down with the fever, regardless of sex or age. Whatever premiss one starts from, there is no reason to conclude that the fever is limited to only one sex, or that despotism is limited to monarchies. Guizot [1787-1874] wrote in his *General History of Civilization in Europe*:

> A monarchy can be instituted in a country like India, which adheres to a caste system, or in a country in which people live together without class distinctions. It may be practiced in a world of despotism and oppression, or in a free and civilized society. A king is a strange kind of head which can be attached to political institutions of different kinds. Or a king is like a strange kind of fruit that can grow on different kinds of political trees.

The above ideas are not novel. They should be well known by intellectuals. But the fact that people still harbor old-fashioned doubts about such things as Christianity and the republican form of government must ultimately be due to a deficiency of impaired vision. If one eye is covered over, the truth appears distorted. People think that equal rights is equivalent to democracy; and that democracy is the same as Christianity, or that Christianity is Western Learning. They are thus misled by their own suppositions and imaginations. Since Mr. Fukuzawa is a scholar of Western learning, they suppose that his views on people's rights must necessarily be Christian or democratic views. And so they have become greatly indignant. If I may use a vulgar example, the owner of a wine shop is not necessarily a drinker, and the master of a *mochi* shop is not necessarily a non-drinker. A person should not immediately judge the inside of a house as he runs by its gate, nor be angry at an owner from just looking at his shop. Though their anger may spring, not from selfishness, but from their sincere patriotism, we can say that they have hearts which are concerned about their country but do not know the proper reasons why.

Postscript
A reporter says that this criticism is precise and piquant.

Appendix
Chronology of Japanese history, with special reference to Fukuzawa Yukichi and *An Encouragement of Learning*

1600–1868	Tokugawa (or Edo) Period
1603	Title of shogun acquired by Ieyasu
1637–38	Shimabara Rebellion: a peasant uprising in Western Kyushu in which many Christians participated.
1639	The last in a series of edicts designed to control contacts between Japan and the outside world is passed. Japanese cannot travel abroad; foreign contacts are limited primarily to trade with Dutch and Chinese ships at Nagasaki, trade with Korea via Tsushima *han*, and smuggling.
1641	Dutch factory moved to Deshima at Nagasaki.
1715	Arai Hakuseki, *Seiyō kibun* (A Report on the Occident) Ogyū Sorai, *Bendō* (Distinguishing the Way); establishment of the Sorai School
1774	Maeno Ryōtaku, Sugita Genpaku, et al., *Kaitai shinsho* (New Book of Anatomy), a Japanese translation of Kulmus' *Ontleedkundige Tafelen* (The original German text is *Anatomische Tabellen*)
1778	Russians arrive at Hokkaido, requesting trade with the Matsumae *han*.
1790	Supremacy of Senior Councilor Matsudaira Sadanobu, who prohibits all teachings except Neo-Confucianism at the Yushima Seidō shrine.
1804	Arrival of Nicholai Rezanov at Nagasaki.
1808	HMS *Phaeton*, Britain's Royal Navy, intrudes into Nagasaki Bay.
1824	Philipp Franz Jonkheer Balthasar von Siebold, German physician and scientist, opens a school in Nagasaki (expelled from Japan in 1829).
1825	Bakufu orders to repel all foreign ships
1835	Fukuzawa Yukichi born in Osaka.
1837	Rice riot in Osaka led by the Confucian scholar Ōshio Heihachirō.
1838	Ogata Kōan opens a school of Western Learning in Osaka.
1839	Painter Watanabe Kazan and physician Takano Chōei, both scholars of Western Learning, incarcerated by the Bakufu.
1853	Arrival of Commodore Perry at Uraga.
1854	Treaty of Kanagawa with the United States.

1858	Treaty of Amity and Commerce with the United States. Fukuzawa opens school of Dutch Learning in Edo (later Tokyo).
1859	Ports of Yokohama, Nagasaki, and Hakodate opened to foreign trade. Fukuzawa starts his study of English.
1860	Fukuzawa joins Japan's first mission to America.
1861	Fukuzawa joins bakufu "foreign ministry" (Gaikokugata) as a translator.
1862	Namamugi Incident (Richardson Incident). Ordered to go to Europe as an official translator for the government, Fukuzawa visits France, England, Holland, Prussia, Russia, and then Portugal.
1863	Bombardment of Shimonoseki.
1865	Imperial ratification of treaties with foreign powers.
1866	Yoshinobu (d. 1913), fifteenth and last shogun. **Conditions in the West** (Vol. 1, 1866; Supplementary Vol., 1868; Vol. II, 1870)
1867	Enthronement of Mutsuhito (later Emperor Meiji). Fukuzawa's second visit to America as attendant to an official delegation to receive delivery of a warship.
1868–1912	**Meiji Period**
1868	January 3, Restoration of Imperial Rule; the separation of Shinto and Buddhism. Fukuzawa ends employment at bakufu "foreign ministry." **Conditions in the West, Outside Volume** (Supplementary Vol.)
1868	ca. May: Fukuzawa names his school Keio-gijuku (later Keio University).
1869	Return of *han* (domain) to the Emperor.
1871	The abolition of the domain and the establishment of prefectures.
1872	Fukuzawa begins the publication of ***An Encouragement of Learning***.
1873	New national military conscription law; new land tax system; establishment of the Home Ministry. 1873–76: The abolition of samurai and their pensioning off.
1874	Public Party of Patriots led by Itagaki Taisuke presents its demand for an elected national assembly.
1875	April: the establishment of the Senate, Supreme Court, and the Assembly of Provincial Governors. June: Japan exchanges with Russia Sakhalin for the Kuriles. October: ***An Outline of a Theory of Civilization***
1877	Satsuma Rebellion takes place.
1878	***Popular Discourse on People's Rights*** ***Popular Discourse on the Rights of Nation***

1879	***On a National Diet***
1880	Fukuzawa founds Kōjunsha (social club).
1881	***A Critique of the Trend of the Times***
1882	Founding of the daily newspaper, ***Jiji Shinpō*** **"On the Imperial House"** ***The Trends of the Times***
1884	Gapsin Coup occurs in Korea; Fukuzawa provides sanctuary for the enlightment reformers, Kim Ok-kyun and Pak Yonghyo.
1885	***On Japanese Women***
1887	Government bans 570 opposition leaders from having residences within three miles of imperial palace.
1888	"On Honoring the Emperor"
1889	Promulgation of the Meiji Constitution.
1890	Promulgation of the Imperial Rescript on Education. First national election held and first Diet convoked. Fukuzawa writes a preface to the reprint of *Dawn of Western Science in Japan* by Sugita Genpaku.
1892	**"The Future of Our National Assembly"**
1894	Sino-Japanese War
1898	Publication of the ***Complete Works of Fukuzawa Yukichi*** in 5 volumes.
1899	***Autobiography*** ***A Critique of* "The Great Learning for Women"** ***The New Great Learning for Women***
1900	***On Moral Code***
1901	Fukuzawa dies at 68.

* Works by Fukuzawa are in boldface.

Fukuzawa Yukichi: Some Representative Writings

a) Pre-Restoration Writings, 1860–69:
  1865 *Tōjin ōrai* (Comings and Goings of the Foreigners)
  1866 *Seiyō jijō* (Conditions in the West; Vol. 1, 1868; Supplementary Vol., 1868; Vol. II, 1870)
  1867 *Seiyō tabi annai* (Guide to Travel in the Western Countries)
  1868 *Kinmō kyūri zukai* (Illustrated Book of the Natural Sciences)
  1869 *Sekai kunizukushi* (All the Countries of the World)

b) Post-Restoration Writings, 1870–1901:
  1872–76 *Gakumon no susume* (An Encouragement of Learning, originally published as seventeen pamphlets)
  1875 *Bunmeiron no gairyaku* (An Outline of a Theory of Civilization)
  1877 *Bunkenron* (On the Division of Power)
  1878 *Tsūzoku minken ron* (Popular Discourse on People's Rights)
   Tsūzoku kokken ron (Popular Discourse on the Rights of Nations)
  1879 *Kokkai ron* (On a National Diet)
  1881 *Jiji shōgen* (A Brief Commentary on the Trends of the Times)
  1882 Founded a daily newspaper, the *Jiji shinpō*, in which many of his writings after 1882 appeared in serial form.
   Jiji taiseiron (The Trends of the Times)
  1885 *Nihon fujinron* (On Japanese Women). Also *Onna daigaku hyōron* (A Critique of "The Great Learning for Women") and *Shin onna daigaku* (The New Great Learning for Women), 1899.
  1888 "Sonnōron" (On Honoring the Emperor)
  1892 "Kokkai no zento" (On the Future of the Diet)
  1897 *Fukuō hyakuwa*, *Fukuō hyakuyowa* (Miscellaneous Essays)
  1898 *Fukuō jiden* (Autobiography, as dictated to a secretary)
  1900 *Shūshin yōryō* (On Moral Code)

Further Reading

Fukuzawa Yukichi. *An Outline of a Theory of Civilization*. The Thought of Fukuzawa Volume 1. Revised translation by David A. Dilworth and G. Cameron Hurst, III. Tokyo: Keio University Press, 2008; New York: Columbia University Press, 2009.

———. *The Autobiography of Yukichi Fukuzawa*. Revised translation by Eiichi Kiyooka with a foreword by Albert M. Craig. New York: Columbia

University Press, 2007.
———. *Fukuzawa Yukichi on Education*. Translated and edited by Eiichi Kiyooka. Tokyo: University of Tokyo Press, 1985.
———. *The Speeches of Fukuzawa: A Translation and Critical Study*. Translated and edited by Wayne H. Oxford. Tokyo: The Hokuseido Press, 1973.
Blacker, Carmen. *The Japanese Enlightenment: A Study of the Writings of Fukuzawa Yukichi*. Cambridge: Cambridge University Press, 1964.
Craig, Albert. "Fukuzawa Yukichi: The Philosophical Foundations of Meiji Nationalism." Reprinted in *The Autobiography of Yukichi Fukuzawa*. New York: Columbia University Press, 2007. 373–429. First published in *Political Development in Modern Japan*. Edited by Robert Ward. Princeton: Princeton University Press, 1968.
———. *Civilization and Enlightenment: The Early Thought of Fukuzawa Yukichi*. Cambridge, MA: Harvard University Press, 2009.
Dilworth, David A. "Was Fukuzawa a Philosopher?" In *Kindai Nihon Kenkyū* (Bulletin of Modern Japanese Studies) 25 (October 2008): 1–26.
Gino K. Piovesana, S. J. *Recent Japanese Philosophical Thought, 1862–1961: A Survey*. Tokyo: Sophia University Press, 1968.
Kosaka Masaaki, ed. *Japanese Thought in the Meiji Era*, trans. and adapted by David Abosch. Tokyo: Pan-Pacific Press, 1958.
Meiroku zasshi: Journal of the Japanese Enlightenment. Translated by William Reynolds. Tokyo: University of Tokyo Press, 1976.
Tamaki Norio. *Yukichi Fukuzawa, 1835–1901: The Spirit of Enterprise in Modern Japan*. Houndmills, Basingstoke: Palgrave, 2001.

INDEX

abacus, xxi, 4, 104
abolition of the *han* (domain) 廃藩, 123
Africa, 6, 20
America, 6, 20, 97
Asano Naganori 浅野長矩 (Asano Takumi-no-kami 浅野内匠頭, 1667–1701), 46, 46*n*
Ashikaga Takauji 足利尊氏 (1305–58)
Asia, xxvii–xxviii, 17, 20, 80, 110
assassination, 17, 47–48, 95, 98, 136

Bakin, Kyokutei (a.k.a. Takizawa Bakin; 滝沢馬琴, 1767–1848), 126, 126*n*
Britain: Great Britain 92; British Parliament, xx
Buddhism, Buddha, xxiv, 17, 109–10, 115

capacity, of men, 5, 9, 12, 32, 60, 73, 136
care 世話, 105
Charles I, 137
Charles II, 137
China, Chinese, the: xxiv, xxviii–xxix, 6, 64, 69, 71, 80–82, 104

Chinese Learning 漢学, xiv–xv, 31, 76
Chōya shinbun 朝野新聞 (Chōya Times), 135*n*, 138
Christianity, xxv, 115, 143–44
civilization: in India, 91; and enlightenment 文明開化, 19, 62; definition of, xxiii, xxv, 57; in France, 130; Japanese, xxiv, 27, 30, 32, 38, 71; modern, 9, 28–29, 38–39, 72, 138–40; progress of, 30, 70, 109, 142; and scholar's role, 41–42; spirit of, 39–40; in Turky, 92; Western, xiv, xviii, xxiii–xxv, 74, 109–113, 116, 138
Clarkson, Thomas (1760–1846), 110
company, 51–53, 97
credulous, credulity (*wakudeki* 惑溺), 110

deception, 29, 94
despotism, 33, 82, 84, 143–44
Diet, the, xxvii, 70, 76, 97
duty 職分: as citizens 46, 51; of the government 43; of scholars 27, 89;

economics, the, xxi, xxix, 5, 41, 73, 89,

107, 11–13
education, 5, 31, 63, 68, 102, 117
England, 6, 22, 27, 97, 107, 110, 116, 142
envy 怨望, 93
equal rights, 32, 77, 144
equality, 16
Europe, xiii, xviii–xix, 20, 138

feudalism, 13–15, 47, 71–73; feudal censors (*metsuke* 目付), 125; feudal lords, 13–15, 83, 96
foreign relations 外国交際 (外交), 5–6, 19, 24, 111, 140, 143
foreigners 27, 38, 53, 75, 81, 140; expulsion of (*jōi* 攘夷), xix, 6; intercourse with, 23–25, 71
Franklin, Benjamin (1706–90), 102, 102n
free trade, 92, 140
freedom: and independence: xxi, xxiv, 5, 12, 74, 85, 137, 199; of the nation xxii, 8, of press 97
Fudō Myō-ō 不動明王, 109

Galileo (1564–1642), 109
Galvani (1737–98), 109
gentlemen: pseudo gentlemen 偽君子, 33
government: Japanese, 6, 33; officials 3, 15, 28, 30–32, 48, 53, 68, 131; service xx, 8, 41, 104 ; tyrannical 17, 54–56, 82, 136. *See also* Tokugawa shogunate
Guizot, François (1787–1874), 144

Heaven 天, xx, 3–4, 12–13, 19, 47, 58; the principle of, xxi, 6–7, 55–56, 60, 62
Hōjō clan 北条, 137, 139, 142
human rights, 13–16,
human sentiment, 56, 96, 139

Hyōgo 兵庫, 141

Imagawa Yoshimoto 今川義元 (1519–60), 22–23
Imperial House 王室, 139–41
independence: of Britain, 27; of Japan, 27–28, 34, 38, 42; national, xxiii, xxv, xxii, 6, 32, 41; personal, xxi, 20; spirit of, 22, 39, 42
Inoue Kakugorō 井上角五郎 (1860–1938), xxviii
international law, 6, 70
Itagaki Taisuke 板垣退助 (1837–1919), 87n

Japan, Japanese: foreign relations, 5–6. 19, 24, 111, 140, 143; independence, 27–28, 34, 38, 42
Jitsugo-kyō 実語教, 3, 3n
Jōdo sect 浄土真宗 (Pure Land Buddhism), 95

Keio-gijuku 慶應義塾 (Keio University), xiii, xx, xxv, 10, 38, 42, 48–49, 135
Kim Ok–kyun 金玉均 (1851–94), xxviii
Kira Yoshihisa 吉良芳央 (Kira Kōzuke-no-suke 吉良上野介, 1641–1702), 46, 46n, 47
Kojiki 古事記 (Record of Ancient Matters), 11, 11n
Korea, xxviii, 71
Kōshū 甲州, 129

lawsuits, 16, 44, 46
learning: practical learning 実学, xxi, 74. *See also* Chinese Learning, Japanese Learnig, Western Learning
Luther, Martin (1483–1546), 110

martyrdom, 136–37

master, and guest 主客, 51, 57–59
Meiji government, 40, 45n, 136
Mencius 孟子, 64–65
middle class, 32–33, 41, 112: women, xxix
Mill, John Stuart (1806–73), 110
Ministry of Education 文部省, 49
monarchy, 143–44
Mongol Court, the, 142
moral subservience (*meibun* 名分), 84–85

Nakatsu 中津, xv–xvii, 9–10, 67, 71, 77
Napoleon III, 23
national seclusion 鎖国, 5–6
newspaper, xiv, xxvii–xxviii, 32, 76, 111, 127, 142
Newton (1642–1727), 109

observation, 88
Oda Nobunaga 織田信長 (1534–82), 22, 22n
Okehazama 桶狭間, 22, 22n
Onna daigaku 女大学 (Great Learning for Women), 62
opening of the ports, xvi–xix, 5, 111
Ōshū Highway 奥州街道, 131, 131n

pagans, 114
parliament, 87
patriotism, 9, 22–23, 47, 83, 104, 136, 142, 144
peasant, 4, 8, 13–16, 47, 61, 104
physics, xvii, 4, 11, 73
political enemy, 46–47
popularity 人望, 125
private punishment 私裁, 44–47
Protestantism, 115
Prussia, xxvi, 23
publication, 32, 42

reasoning, 88

reciprocity, 16
reformer, 33
relief laws (England), 107
religion, 115, 143; Roman, 110, 115
retainer: forty-seven retainers of the Akō 赤穂の義士, 46, 84, 138; loyal retainer, 忠臣義士, 57–58, 83, 136–38

samurai: ex-samurai 士族, xxv, 8, 23, 123. *See also* retainer
scholars, 11, 42, 72, 76, 88–89; belonged to the middle class, 41; of Chinese Learning, 31, 62; of Confucian Learning, 4; and government, 31, 35, 49; of Japanese Learning, 4, 31, 62; of Western Learning, 31–32, 73–74, 88, 144
science, xv, xxiv, 4–5
Shinran 親鸞, 115–16
slaves, 6, 110
Smith, Adam (1723–90), 41
society, 14, 16, 76–77, 93–96, 125, 127: classes of, 4, 8, 28; in Japan, xxix–xxx; and nation, 19; and people, 68–69, 98, 119; reforms in, 32; uncivilized, 57
Spain, 138
speech 演説, 87, 123, 128–30
spirit: of civilization, 38–40; of independence, 22, 39, 42; of the times, 41–42
statistics, 97
Stephenson, George (1781–1848), 41
Sugita Genpaku 杉田玄白 (1733–1817), 71, 71n
Suruga 駿河, 22, 22n, 23

Takeda clan, the 武田, 137–38
terakoya 寺子屋 (temple school), xxi, xxiv, 3n
Tōkaidō 東海道, 7, 7n, 88

Tokugawa shogunate 徳川幕府, xx, xxiv, 7, 14–15, 24–25, 46
Tokyo prefecture, the, 49
townsfolk 町人, 4, 14–16, 24, 33, 47, 83, 85
trend of the times, x, 41

Uesugi clan, the 上杉, 137–38

Watt, James (1736–1819), 41
Wayland, Francis (1796–1865), xx*n*, 59, 136
Western Learning, xvi, 31–32, 71–74, 88–89, 104, 144; Fukuzawa's commitment to, xix, xxiv
women: Fukuzawa on, xiv, xxvii, xxix, 5, 62–63, 114–16; Mill on, 110

Yokohama 横浜, xviii, 24

Zen, 59, 89
Zhou dynasty 唐, 62, 81

TRANSLATOR

David A. Dilworth (1934-) is Professor of Philosophy at the State University of New York, Stony Brook. He earned his Ph.D.s from Fordham University and Columbia University. His publication includes *Philosophy in World Perspective: A Comparative Hermeneutic of the Major Theories* (Yale University Press, 1989), *Sourcebook for Modern Japanese Philosophy: Selected Documents* (editor; Greenwood, 1998), translations of Fukuzawa's *An Encouragement of Learning* (with Hirano Umeyo; Sophia University Press, 1969) and Nishida Kitaro's *Last Writings: Nothingness and the Religious Worldview* (University of Hawaii Press, 1987).

CONTRIBUTOR

Nishikawa Shunsaku (西川俊作 1932–2010) was Professor Emeritus at Keio University, and former Director of the Fukuzawa Memorial Center for Modern Japanese Studies, Keio University. His publication includes *Keizai gaku* (On Economics, 4th edition; Toyo Keizai, 1994), *Fukuzawa Yukichi no yokogao* (True Face of Fukuzawa Yukichi; Keio University Press, 1998), and the posthumously published work, *Chōshū no Keizai kōzō* (Political Structure of Chōshū domain; ed. Saito Osamu. Toyo Keizai, 2012).

慶應義塾創立150年記念
THE THOUGHT OF FUKUZAWA

編集顧問 Advisory Board
Albert M. Craig
安西祐一郎 Anzai Yūichirō
福澤武 Fukuzawa Takeshi
服部禮次郎 Hattori Reijirō
坂本達哉 Sakamoto Tatsuya

編集委員 Editorial Committee
Helen Ballhatchet
池田幸弘 Ikeda Yukihiro
岩谷十郎 Iwatani Jūrō
小室正紀 Komuro Masamichi
西川俊作 Nishikawa Shunsaku
西澤直子 Nishizawa Naoko
山内慶太 Yamauchi Keita

The Thought of Fukuzawa, Volume 2

An Encouragement of Learning

2012年4月30日 初版第1刷発行
2025年1月10日 初版第2刷発行

著　者――――福澤諭吉
訳　者――――David A. Dilworth
解　題――――西川俊作
発行者――――坂上　弘
発行所――――慶應義塾大学出版会株式会社
　　　　　　〒108-8346 東京都港区三田2-19-30
　　　　　　TEL〔編集部〕03-3451-0931
　　　　　　　　〔営業部〕03-3451-3584〈ご注文〉
　　　　　　　　〔 〃 〕03-3451-6926
　　　　　　FAX〔営業部〕03-3451-3122
　　　　　　振替　00190-8-155497
　　　　　　http://www.keio-up.co.jp/
ブックデザイン――宮川なつみ
印刷・製本――――大日本印刷株式会社

©2012 Keio University Press
Printed in Japan ISBN 978-4-7664-1684-8

慶應義塾大学出版会

The Thought of Fukuzawa Vol. 1

An Outline of a Theory of Civilization

福澤諭吉 著
デヴィッド・A・ディルワース／G・キャメロン・ハースト, Ⅲ 訳

福澤の思索力が最も充実した壮年期の著作（1875年刊行）で、最高傑作の一つと名高い『文明論之概略』の英訳。近代日本を啓蒙し、先導した福澤諭吉の著作を、国内外の読者に向けて英訳で刊行するシリーズの第1巻。＊年表・参考文献一覧・索引付き。

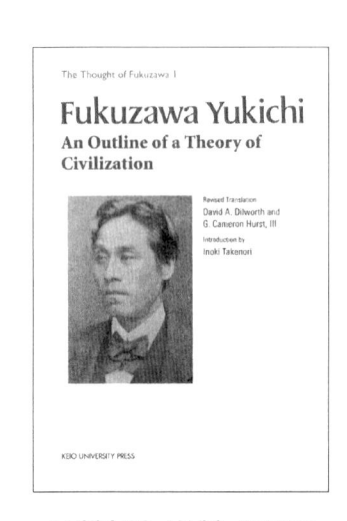

B5判変型／並製／320頁
ISBN 978-4-7664-1560-5
●3200円

表示価格は刊行時の本体価格（税別）です。